THE MENACE OF OVERPRODUCTION

ITS CAUSE, EXTENT AND CURE

THE MENACE OF OVERPRODUCTION

ITS CAUSE, EXTENT AND CURE

EDITED BY
SCOVILLE HAMLIN

Essay Index Reprint Series

BOOKS FOR LIBRARIES PRESS
FREEPORT, NEW YORK

First Published 1930
Reprinted 1969

STANDARD BOOK NUMBER:
8369-1295-0

LIBRARY OF CONGRESS CATALOG CARD NUMBER:
76-93344

PRINTED IN THE UNITED STATES OF AMERICA

ACKNOWLEDGMENT

———

THE editor extends his grateful thanks to Mr. P. Everett Lockhart and Miss Grace Lockhart for their sincere interest and assistance in the preparation of this book.

The encouragement and aid given by Mr. Nelson M. Brooks enlist my gratitude.

Additional thanks are due Mr. Stuart Chase for his constructive criticism and advice.

FOREWORD

THE Machine Age has presented us with a great variety of new products fabricated with an unheard-of ingenuity and efficiency. But it has also deposited on our doorsteps certain grave problems of adjustment to these billion odd horses of mechanical energy now running in tangents more or less unchecked and untamed. Of all problems none are more immediately pressing than overproduction and its twin, unemployment. The two are inseparably linked. One demoralizes us with the burden of idle plant and capital, the other with idle men and women. This book is extraordinarily timely. It gives us first the facts as to the extent of overproduction—defined primarily as plant capacity in excess of market demands—in many fields, competently summarized by experts. Secondly, it gives us many valuable hints and suggestions for constructive action. Symposiums are all too frequently unwieldy documents, but in approaching this particular menace of the Machine Age, a symposium, it seems to me, is an apt and logical vehicle. We receive not one student's view with its inevitable personal bias, but the composite view of many able specialists, each dealing with that aspect of industry which he knows as he knows his own profit and loss account. The result is unity in diversity. Each contributor has his own special problem but all unite in condemning the waste, loss, friction, and great financial burden of more machines, more capital equipment, than can be effectively utilized under present economic conditions. I never encountered a more unanimous chorus. The situation holds in fat years, as well as lean, and appears to be growing progressively worse with the advance of the technical arts. The effect of idle machines on idle men, and the consequent appalling human waste and loss, is only too clearly indicated. I hope this book will be widely read, its facts assimilated, and its constructive suggestions sifted, and if necessary added to, for bold and immediate action.

STUART CHASE

New York City

CONTENTS

THE MENACE OF OVERPRODUCTION

I

THE COST OF OVERPRODUCTION IN THE BITUMINOUS MINING INDUSTRY

By C. E. BOCKUS

President, National Coal Association

THERE is general agreement on the economic principle that the overproduction of a commodity involves waste of capital, labor and natural resources. To produce more of a commodity than consumers want or can buy is no less wasteful than would be the production of a commodity for which consumers had no use at all. These generalizations apply to the bituminous mining industry, but there are two special characteristics of the industry that should be borne in mind in discussing the question raised by the title of this article.

In the first place, strictly speaking, there is no such thing as actual overproduction of bituminous coal over any considerable period of time. It is only under unusual conditions that bituminous coal is mined before it is sold. Occasionally there is real overproduction of particular sizes of coal because of a profitable demand for other sizes, the production of which involves the making of sizes for which there is no immediate market. Occasionally a mine is kept in operation for a short period in spite of lack of orders, because the operator hopes and expects to find a market for his product in the near future, but in the aggregate the unsold coal produced under either of these conditions constitutes a small percentage of the total output.

It is worth noting in passing, however, that even this small amount of actual overproduction has serious market consequences. This is due to the nature of the demand for bituminous coal. That demand is what economists call inelastic, that is, whether for domestic heating or for industrial purposes, consumers need and must have a definite amount of coal. No price concessions will induce them to buy more than they need and no advance in price within reasonable limits will bring about an appreciable decline in the amount consumed. As a result of these conditions, even a small amount of unsold coal shipped into any particular market will have a demoralizing effect on prices in that market until this "distress coal" is disposed of.

However, such actual overproduction, as pointed out above, is only occasional and incidental. The real problem of the industry arises from the existence of excess capacity, that is, capacity to produce coal in excess of the demand for the product. Such excess capacity undoubtedly exists, but it is not easy to measure its extent, due to the difficulty of determining the base from which the excess is to be measured.

Even in a normal year, that is, a year unaffected by labor or transportation difficulties or unusual demand from any source, the weekly production of bituminous coal varies, in round numbers, from 7,000,000 to 12,000,000 tons. A 7,000-000 ton weekly output is at the rate of 364,000,000 tons a year, while a 12,000,000 ton output is at the rate of 624,000,000 tons a year. This seasonal irregularity of operation is entirely due to the coal consumers. Coal operators would prefer uniformity of operation throughout the year. Such uniformity would be more profitable to them as well as more economical in the long run to society. Experience has shown that the operators can do little to remedy the situation. Neither seasonal changes in prices nor seasonal changes in freight rates, both of which devices have been suggested, hold out promise of material relief. Influenced by the cost of storing a bulky commodity like bituminous coal, it is difficult to induce a consumer to increase his summer purchases appreciably by any reasonable concession in the cost of his fuel. For a long period he has always been able to obtain the coal he wants when he wants it—an added argument to him for not filling his bin in summer.

If consumers are going to ask for 12,000,000 tons of coal a week during a period of the year, mining capacity capable of producing that coal can hardly be regarded as excessive. Even on the basis of seasonal fluctuations alone, it is evident that the idea of eliminating excess capacity is visionary. For many months in the year at the best the industry must learn to live and prosper with unused coal-mining capacity.

But secular changes in the demand for bituminous coal may at times bring about a demand even greater than the normal winter figure. In time of war, as illustrated by our recent experience, we may need to produce far greater amounts than in normal peace times. The output of bituminous coal for the year 1918, stimulated by war demand, amounted to approximately 579,000,000 tons, a total that has never been equalled since. As the opening of new coal mines is a matter involving considerable periods of time, a certain amount of capacity in excess of normal demands may well be regarded as an essential form of preparation for emergencies.

Even in times of peace, demand frequently rises to unusual peaks. In fact the greatest single week's output was produced not during the war but in 1926, during the last British strike. In one week in that year 14,551,000 tons were produced. The demand was even greater, the limiting factor being the ability of the piers to load coal for export. Unless we are to take the position that in such periods we are to be indifferent to

the needs of consumers, the capacity required to produce
14,500,000 tons a week, a rate of more than 750,000,000 tons
a year, cannot properly be regarded as excess capacity. But
provision for meeting unusually heavy demands of this sort
involves a further amount of unused mining capacity during
normal periods.

I have developed these ideas at considerable length in order
to emphasize the point that, as stated above, the problem
facing the bituminous mining industry is not that of eliminating excess capacity but that of devising some method of
operation and control which will enable the industry to live
and prosper in spite of such unused capacity. The unused
capacity is a social necessity. It is unreasonable and intolerable
that the industry should be made to bear the entire burden
of maintaining such capacity with its depressing effect upon
price and upon the profit of operation.

There are no reliable figures showing the capacity of the
bituminous mines of the United States. One method of ar-
riving at an estimate of such capacity is to increase the actual
production, as reported by the Bureau of Mines, by an amount
representing the potential output of idle days. Thus, in 1928,
using round figures, 500,000,000 tons were produced in 200
days. If the mines had worked at the same rate for 300 days
in the year they would have produced 750,000,000 tons of
coal, an amount almost identical with the actual rate of production in the one week referred to above. On that assumption there was no unused mining capacity in the country in
the week of December 4, 1926. However, it must be recognized that the figure for capacity arrived at in this way, for
reasons that I need not develop, is too low, and that even in
that week there was mine capacity for a further increase in
production. But from my point of view that question is of
little importance, for whether the total capacity is more or
less in excess of the maximum demand, the industry, if it is

to be prepared to meet its social exigencies, must operate for 90 per cent of the time with unused mining capacity.

In one respect the bituminous mining industry has had to meet unusually trying conditions during the last decade. A brief review of the history of the industry brings out in a striking way the fact that for many decades its market increased as rapidly as or even more rapidly than the rate of increase in the industrial life of the nation. Under such circumstances the problem before the industry was that of expanding its capacity rapidly enough to meet the increasing demand.

How different has been the story since the war! During the eleven years from 1919 to 1929, inclusive, there has been no year in which the production of bituminous coal has equalled that of 1918. The average annual output for the three years 1917-1918-1919 amounted to 532,000,000 net tons, while during the three years 1927-1928-1929 it was only 517,-000,000 tons. In other words, an industry that had acquired the habit of expanding to meet a constantly increasing demand has during the last decade seen no increase in such demand. During this same period the industrial life of the country has gone through a period of development unprecedented in its history.

The reasons for this failure of bituminous coal consumption to keep pace with the expansion of industry have been frequently pointed out and I need do no more than refer to them briefly. There has been the encroachment of substitute fuels upon fields once nearly monopolized by coal; improvements in methods and devices for preparing and burning coal have been made which have increased its efficiency and correspondingly reduced the quantity required to develop a given amount of power; and finally the improvements of countless kinds in the mechanical equipment of industry which have curtailed the consumption of power in many industrial operations. While all these influences were felt more or less before the war, their development since that time has been at a pace that has brought about a real revolution in the fuel situation. The chief competitors of bituminous coal are petroleum and its products, natural gas and hydro-generated electricity. The effect of the competition of these rival sources of heat and power has been felt alike in the household and in the field of industry.

The relative rate of growth of coal, petroleum, natural gas, and water power as sources of energy in the United States since 1918 is best shown by the figures published by the Bureau of Mines in its recent "Bituminous Coal Tables." From that publication it appears that if the consumption of each source of energy in the year 1918 is represented as 100, the consumption for the year 1928 would be represented by the following index numbers: bituminous coal—86; petroleum —249; natural gas—218; water power—232. However, it must not be forgotten that even in 1928 bituminous coal furnished 53 per cent of the total energy derived from mineral fuels and water power.

A computation utilizing the terms of equivalence set forth in the Bureau of Mines' report shows that in 1918 oil, gas, and water were generating power whose production would have required the consumption of 152,000,000 tons of bituminous coal. By 1928 the consumption of substitutes had increased to the equivalent of 372,000,000 tons of bituminous coal. In other words, by the end of that period the encroachment of rival sources of power had kept the bituminous mining industry out of a yearly market for 220,000,000 tons of its product more than it had lost in 1918. It is true that these figures include the consumption of fuel in forms in which coal could not be used directly, such as the consumption of gasoline in internal combustion engines. However, even for such purposes coal and the products of the distillation of coal might be utilized if economic conditions ever justified the resort to coal distillation.

The second development affecting the demand for bituminous coal has been the improvement in methods of coal utilization. These improvements have taken many forms and have been of wide application, but the degree to which they have been carried is capable of exact measurement in only a few lines of consumption. Information is particularly complete with respect to the use of coal as locomotive fuel and the use of coal in the generation of electric power.

In 1918 public utility plants consumed on the average 3.35 pounds of coal per kilowatt-hour of output. In 1928 the consumption had been reduced to 1.76 pounds. If the 1928 output had been produced at the 1918 rate of coal consumption, there would have been a market for nearly 40,000,000 tons of bituminous coal more than was actually required. Similarly, in the case of the railroads, in 1918 it required the consumption of 174 pounds of coal to move 1000 tons of freight and equipment one mile; in 1928 this amount had been reduced to 127 pounds. If the 1928 load had been moved at the 1918 rate of consumption, it would have required 25,000,000 additional tons of coal. Similar economies in passenger and other forms of service would account for another saving of some 15,000,000 tons, showing a total saving in railroad transportation due to improved methods of coal combustion and improved railway equipment totalling some 40,000,000 tons.

While definite figures are not available for many other lines of industrial consumption, it is well known that the movement toward more efficient combustion has been widespread. It is a conservative assumption that economies in those other lines have reduced coal consumption by 35,000,000 tons, making a total loss of market in all these lines of industry of 112,000,000 tons. This 112,000,000 tons a year, lost on account of increased efficiency of consumption, must be added to the 220,000,000 tons per year, which would have been consumed but for the utilization of rival sources of power, to obtain a complete picture of the status of the market for coal in recent years. This combination of circumstances answers the question raised earlier in this paper as to why the demand for bituminous coal has remained practically stationary during a decade of rapid industrial expansion.

The adaptation of capacity to demand made necessary by these developments has been going on in the bituminous-mining industry, and probably would have been fairly well worked out had it not been for a disturbing factor furnished by the labor situation. For several years organized labor in the industry succeeded in perpetuating in certain fields an abnormally high wage scale adopted at the time of the maximum cost of living following the war. With that scale in existence in the union fields, the non-union fields found an opportunity to encroach upon the existing markets of the union operators. This situation caused an expansion of capacity in the non-union territory within reach of these markets, which otherwise might not have been developed. The condition causing such sectional development no longer exists and the condition of excess capacity thereby brought about is undergoing readjustment.

Even during this period of readjustment, capacity additions are being made to bituminous-mining properties, and that in two ways. In the first place, there are always a certain number of companies either opening up new mines or enlarging the capacity of existing mines, because they believe that they enjoy special advantages which will enable them to operate at a profit, even under existing market conditions. No record has been kept of such expansion of capacity, but not infrequently the trade press carries notices of such new or enlarged enterprises.

The other method by which mine capacity is expanding is

through the extension of mine mechanization. This general term covers a variety of developments, and the degree of progress varies for different forms of mechanization. Underground haulage is now largely mechanical. The percentage undercut by hand has declined from 23.8 in 1918 to 14.2 in 1928. Mechanical loaders were not in use in 1918. In 1923 only 1,880,000 tons were reported as loaded by such devices. In 1928 the amount had increased to 14,559,000 tons, and the rate of increase shows no indication of declining. It is impossible to give any definite measurement of the increased capacity of mines created by the adoption of mechanical devices, but that influence is undoubtedly reflected in the fact that between 1918 and 1928 the average output per day per man employed increased from 3.78 tons to 4.73 tons, a gain of 25 per cent. The influence of mechanical loaders upon output per man has only begun to be felt.

The effect of mine mechanization will not be confined to the resulting increase in mine capacity. Not all mines can be adapted to mechanical production. Not only must there be sufficient room for machines to work efficiently, but the roof must be fairly firm to insure safety and the coal must be free from partings or other impurities so that it can be loaded directly from the face. Finally, since mechanical equipment is expensive, the operation must be on a sufficiently large scale to justify the investment. When it is considered that in 1928 only 2185 mines, or approximately one-third of the 6450 mines in operation, produced more than 50,000 tons a year, it will be realized that there is a definite limit to the extent to which complete mine mechanization can be profitably adopted.

As mine mechanization can be applied only to mines of some size, and as its effect is to increase the capacity of such mines, the result of the mine mechanization movement will be a tendency toward the elimination of small mines and the concentration of coal production in fewer and larger companies.

Such increase in the size of operating units should have a direct bearing upon the possibility of applying remedies to the existing condition of price depression. It will reenforce the already existing advantages of large-scale operation which bituminous mining shares with many other industries.

So far as its effect upon price is concerned, there is perhaps little to choose between overcapacity and overproduction. It is the existence of overcapacity and the lack of adequate methods of counteracting its effect, which has been responsible for the unsatisfactory economic condition in which the industry finds itself. The unrestrained effort of individual operators to utilize their own capacity when conditions of the market make it certain that large amounts of capacity must go unutilized, has driven the price of bituminous coal down to its present unprofitable level.

There are two authoritative sources of information with respect to the average price of coal. The Bureau of Mines compiles annually a figure representing the average realization received by mine operators for all coal produced. *Coal Age* publishes an annual figure for the average spot price on board railroad cars at the mine of coal sold commercially. Both of these indexes record a sharp and substantial decline in price over the period from 1918 to 1929, inclusive. The movement can be best followed by considering the average annual price by three-year periods.

In the case of the Bureau of Mines' realization figure, the result was as follows: 1918, 1919, and 1920—$2.94; 1921, 1922, and 1923—$2.88; 1924, 1925, and 1926—$2.10; 1927 and 1928 (1929 not yet available)—$1.93. The average *Coal Age* spot price for the same periods was $3.60, $2.99, $2.12, and $1.86, the last average including the year 1929.

The only explanation of this price decline is to be found in the fact that the operator has been passing along to the consumer every cent of the economy of operation made possible either by wage readjustments, by declines in the cost of material, or by more efficient methods of operation. This record indicates that so long as the effect of the pressure of excess mine capacity remains unrelieved, there is little hope for any substantial improvement in the financial condition of the industry as a whole. As rapidly as more economical methods of production can be extended to a sufficient proportion of the mine capacity of the country, the entire gain from such economical operation accrues to the benefit of consumers in the form of lower prices.

The uneconomical prices at which bituminous coal is sold have certain harmful effects upon bituminous mine operation. Those effects are so obvious and at the same time so incapable of definite measurement, that I need do no more than briefly enumerate them. In the first place, capital is not inclined to enter an industry unless its future is promising. Under existing conditions it is not always easy for even substantial mining enterprises to obtain the full amount of capital necessary for the most economical operation. This difficulty in obtaining credit, together with the close margin on which the industry operates, has been a serious obstacle in the way of the development by the industry itself of broad fundamental research work into methods of coal production on the one hand and coal utilization on the other hand.

Moreover, it must be recognized that the close margin of profit on which bituminous mines must operate makes it difficult to obtain the highest class of managerial ability, which is slow to enter an industry in which the future is uncertain. Similarly, the tendency of such a condition is to depress wages. The most humanitarian operator often finds himself in a situation in which he must put it up to his men to choose between no work and work at a wage which will enable him to book orders for his product. Finally, it is probably true in some instances that economic pressure prevents operators from adopting and installing safety measures and devices, even though they realize that in the long run such devices are desirable, not only from humanitarian but also from financial considerations.

From the social point of view the mining industry occupies a different position from that of an ordinary manufacturing establishment because it is dealing with a natural resource of definitely limited supply. The building and equipping of shoe factories with a capacity in excess of demand involves a waste of only a part of the capital and labor required for such construction. When the shoe factory is abandoned the buildings and some of the equipment can be utilized for other purposes. The net loss is represented by only so much of the investment as has no such extraneous use.

The opening and equipping of an unneeded mining property involves the same kind of loss, but in addition entails two other forms of serious social harm. In the first place, the abandonment of a coal mine after it has been in operation for any length of time usually means the permanent loss of the unmined coal, for after the most accessible and most easily mined coal has been removed, it is in most cases economically unprofitable to attempt to mine the more distant and more costly reserves. Abandoning a coal mine is frequently abandoning the unmined coal.

In the second place, the low prices resulting from such uneconomical mine development lead to waste in the mining of coal. Low prices impose a limit upon the percentage of coal recovered in mine operation. They advance the point at which increasing costs of recovery are met by mine realization, beyond which recovery cannot be economically carried. It is doubtful whether there is any other industry in which the supposed advantage of unrestricted competition in assuring low prices to consumers is offset by so many and so serious social losses.

How is the situation to be remedied? How is the industry to be enabled to maintain the mine capacity needed to meet emergency demand and at the same time secure a price for its product adequate to enable it to operate most advantageously, to maintain the standard of earnings of its workers and to yield a reasonable return to the capital invested? The European method of meeting this situation is through the establishment of cartels. These cartels operate under legal sanction and are intended to so allocate the market for coal as among different producers and so regulate price at which it sells as to assure those participating in the industry a fair and reasonable return, and at the same time avoid the social wastes incident to our unrestricted competitive policy.

It is to be noted that these cartels follow the very practices specifically condemned by the Sherman and Clayton Acts, namely, the regulation of output and price and the division of territory; and that they follow these practices without incurring the charge of undue exploitation of the consumers of their product. Such organized self-control of the industry is impossible in this country so long as the prohibitions of the Sherman and Clayton Acts are held to apply to industries exploiting natural resources.

Being deprived of the right to practice adequate self-regulation, the industry is attempting to improve conditions as far as possible through cooperative agreements to abandon harmful practices. These agreements are embodied in codes of ethics. Through the machinery of trade practice conferences, such codes may secure a certain amount of legal standing by submission to the Federal Trade Commission. The Commission classifies the practices approved or condemned by the industry in two groups. In the first group it places those unfair practices that in its belief have already received, directly or by implication, judicial condemnation as violations of law. In the second group it places those practices which, while not falling under the condemnation of positive law, are yet held to be harmful in their effects upon the economic welfare of the industry and the public. By the adoption of such codes of ethics and their observance some restraint may be placed upon the cut-throat competitive practices of an industry. However, so long as the anti-trust laws remain unchanged, nothing can be embodied in those codes which provides for either the cooperative regulation of production or prices, or for any division of territory. And as it has been stated, these are the very practices on which the success of the European cartels is based.

The precise need of the industry is the right to secure, by cooperative action, the continuous adjustment of the production of bituminous coal to the existing demand for it, thereby discouraging wasteful methods of production and consumption and making possible its production under conditions that will insure the welfare of its employees and the prosperity of its operating companies. The fear that such limited powers could be abused to the detriment of industry and society is entirely unfounded. It could not work that way in the United States, because of the enormous acreage of coal deposits in this country and the large number of companies engaged in mining operations. As George Otis Smith, Director U. S. Geological Survey, pointed out years ago, nature itself has made impossible the exploiting of consumers of bituminous coal through monopolistic combinations.

II

OVERPRODUCTION IN THE OIL INDUSTRY

By E. P. SALISBURY
Statistician, Standard Oil Co. (N. J.)

STATISTICS of the growth of the petroleum industry, while impressive in themselves, are only a counterpart in larger dimensions of the history of many other American commercial developments. If petroleum has a distinguishing feature, it is that ever since its discovery it has met unexpected requirements with unfailing efficiency and has made possible one of the greatest of industrial revolutions—the common use of the internal combustion engine. At some time or other, labor disturbances, inadequacy of supplies, or other causes have interrupted the free use of many other commodities, but even the epochal demands of the Great War failed to result in any serious inconvenience to the consumers of petroleum.

In its brief but amazingly rapid growth, the industry has been signally free from any appreciable degree of physical waste. Its foundations were laid upon principles of economical operation and the creation of wealth through the development of all the possibilities of petroleum as a commercial product, rather than upon a system aiming at quick and large profits. The pioneers in petroleum were not pioneers in that alone, but also in the application of the principle of order to all industry. From the orgy of overproduction which followed the completion of the first oil well by Col. Drake, physical loss in the production, transportation, and manufacture of petroleum products has been probably materially lower than that of practically any other basic industry and this avoidance of waste still continues to be attributable to high scientific attainment and the necessity of the severest economies as essential to existence.

Each chapter in the story of petroleum is prefaced by a prophecy of the doom of the industry. With striking regularity since its discovery, there have appeared pronouncements, backed by the most authoritative data, to the effect that the world's reserves of petroleum had been definitely plotted and that, at the current rate of consumption, these reserves would be entirely exhausted in a given period of years. With equal regularity, the industry has confounded these prophets by new discoveries which have indefinitely postponed the date of the industry's extinction, until now the reserves of petroleum and commercial substitutes which will be available in the event of complete depletion of petroleum have been so definitely established as to render futile any effort to forecast a period of insufficient supply.

Even ten years ago the user of gasoline could not believe that the yield of this product from crude could be greatly increased, nor was it realized that the industry was but on the threshold of the science of the discovery and development of petroliferous formations. In these and other directions, the industry has manifested an amazing, and now somewhat disconcerting ingenuity, the result of which is that in these ten years it has practically continuously overproduced crude and its principal product, gasoline. It has placed itself in the position of a merchant who carries upon his shelves goods largely in excess of his annual turnover.

The recent overproduction of petroleum undoubtedly has its genesis in the efforts put forth by the industry to meet war requirements. The eyes of the whole world were then focussed upon the extraordinary value of petroleum to civilization, and enormous amounts of capital were diverted from other uses to employment in some phase or other of the oil business. New petroleum enterprises were founded by thousands, and the rapid and widespread utilization of motor transportation and the new commercial uses which were continually being found for petroleum products in the great majority of cases justified these investments. Against what appeared to be insatiable markets, oil fields hitherto unknown were discovered and developed upon a gigantic scale. Processes of refining were revolutionized to the extent that one barrel of the raw product in reserve became as great a protection against the future as two barrels had been a few years previous.

In 1910 the world industry produced slightly under 900,000 barrels of crude oil every day. By 1920 it had increased this daily production to 1,900,000 barrels and in the year just past it created a new record of over 4,000,000 barrels per day. Supplementary to this, what is known as shut-in production, by which is meant the additional amount of crude which could be produced if all existing wells were operated to maximum capacity, rose to about 1,950,000 barrels daily. In other words the industry, with a market of 4,000,000 barrels daily, is carrying an overhead based upon actual and shut-in production of 5,950,000 barrels per day—more than 48 per cent above its existing requirements. Moreover, if the incentive existed to realize the full gasoline content of every barrel, an even smaller production would suffice. Even these figures do not fully picture the extent to which overproduction has carried us, for another factor in the situation is that additional drilling in fields already proven would rapidly result in an even greater producing capacity.

With daily production nearly always exceeding consumption, above ground storage has been continuously increasing and during the last seven years there has been accumulated above ground in the United States alone about 305,000,000 barrels of crude and products. In only one of the years named was there any draft on these stocks. This accumulation has taken place in spite of the efforts of the Federal Oil Conservation Board and the petroleum industry itself to curtail production to a point where demand and supply would be more nearly in balance.

About 70 per cent of the income of the oil industry is derived from gasoline, and in the manufacture of sufficient gasoline a sufficiency of other products is a natural consequence. As a matter of fact, fuel oil has been largely overproduced in order to take care of the current overproduction of crude. The overproduction of fuel oil has forced its price far below its equivalent value to coal on a thermal basis and the employment of such fuel oil to the exclusion of coal in a large percentage is a waste of potential gasoline and probably the greatest economic waste chargeable to the industry. Parenthetically, it might be stated that the physical loss in production, transportation, and manufacture of petroleum and its products is probably materially lower than that of most basic industries, the avoidance of physical waste being due to high scientific attainment and necessity under extreme competition of the severest economies as essential to existence.

Competitive drilling is one of the fundamental causes of overproduction. The fugitive nature of oil deposits and the legal requirements governing rights to oil leases both are incentives to this practice. Most leases enjoin prompt drilling under penalty of forfeiture, and jurisprudence demands that when wells enter production on one property the lessee of the adjoining property must produce oil in a reasonable and diligent manner or else forfeit the lease. These conditions have been incentives to an unreasoning competition on the part of each lessee to obtain the maximum production from his own lease. He knows that he must reach the oil sands quickly and produce as large a volume as possible or else the oil which lies below his property will flow to his neighbor. In his efforts he has but one consideration—to procure maximum production promptly—and he has little thought for methods which would conserve the gas energy in the field and permit of a lower production cost over a period of time as well as actually increasing the total yield from the field. Unit operation of oil fields, it has been demonstrated where such policy has been applied, is the only solution to this problem, and a great deal of effort has been made to obtain unit operation. At the present time, however, a small minority of operators or even one non-concurring operator can prevent unit operation in a pool.

Overproduction of gasoline is more detrimental to the economic results of the industry than the overproduction of crude alone. Furthermore, from a legal as well as a practical standpoint, it is much more difficult to balance refinery operations to gasoline demand than it is to balance crude oil production to its demand. Up to the present time the greatest progress made in this direction has been through the improvement in the preparation and dissemination of statistical information on the gasoline situation. The only strong influence to keep gasoline production within bounds at the present time appears to be through education of the refiners and the more prompt availability of information on the trend of gasoline consumption, manufacture, and stocks.

The remarkable advance in scientific refining practice which past years have witnessed, with its stimulus to drilling activities contributing to petroleum overproduction, has represented a competition of brains as well as of capital. Had the refining industry stood still during the past decade, it would not now be burdened with surplus products nor with the enormous cost of reconstruction of refining equipment, which has represented a practically continuous expenditure in that time. The economic benefits to the present and future consumer of petroleum products have been incalculable, but the industry has for the time penalized itself by its own genius. With overproduction of the raw material and with capital readily available to petroleum enterprises, it was a natural sequence that there should come into existence a surplus of refining capacity as well as of marketing and distributing facilities. The average motorist is impressed by the fact that practically no commodity he buys is made so conveniently available to him as gasoline, and realizes that the cost of the capital represented by the multitude of unnecessary service stations must be borne by someone. He probably does not comprehend that behind the service station are investments of larger magnitude in equally unnecessary refining equipment and production operation. The cost of this capital is, of course, borne by the consumer of the industry's products and by the hundreds of thousands of investors who have provided this capital. An inadequate return is inevitable while overproduction of crude and overconstruction of facilities exist, for, before dividends, the industry must provide out of its earnings for its own perpetuation and for the depletion of its physical resources, which, however abundant at the present, must diminish some time. The research which has already provided a commercial substitute for petroleum, if and when such becomes necessary, has represented years of effort and involves huge expenditures of capital. The marked improvement in products has only been accomplished by expensive experiments and the creation and construction of new equipment. Added to this is, of course, the provision that must be made to amortize the cost of the enormous petroleum plant which some day, years hence, will be idle.

Overproduction in all phases of the oil business has been due not alone to the glamour which the prospect of "striking oil" undoubtedly possesses for many people, but to the circumstance that participation in the business is comparatively easy, even for those of little capital. An investment in a comparatively moderate-priced lease has always the possibilities of the birth of one or more petroleum corporations. An insignificant amount, as compared with the investment necessary in almost any other business, will bring a new service station into existence overnight. A man with sufficient funds to pay the rent of premises for a month and with credit with an oil company can be a member of the oil industry at will. There is no more striking contrast furnished by modern commerce than that of the histories of the petroleum industry and of its most closely allied industry, the manufacture of motor cars. The petroleum industry was launched and directed for years by a comparatively small group of men, but since that time the consuming markets have been shared each year by a vastly and steadily increasing number of units. Fast as petroleum markets have grown, the number of those entering the business of purveying to these markets has multiplied more rapidly. The trend in motor-car manufacture has been entirely in the opposite direction. With the advent of the motor car, every wagon shop was a potential motor-car factory. The history of that industry has been one of elimination, and today the survivors constitute only a small percentage of those who, thirty years ago, started in the race. A motor magazine, even as late as fifteen years ago, contains the names of dozens of makes of motors which are only memories today.

Competition in the oil business, as in every other industry, will regulate itself, but as it is at present organized, its earnings cannot be sufficient without a larger measure of cooperative effort in the balancing of production and demand. In the last few years some progress has been made in this direction, and if this progress can be maintained, the industry may arrive at a fair return upon its capital through the avoidance of wasteful production and the reduction of excessive stocks now above ground. It seems inconceivable, and it certainly is undesirable, that an industry of such magnitude, concerned with the manufacture and distribution of products so essential to public welfare, should go through a period of intense uneconomic competition.

III

FACTORS IN RESTORING EQUILIBRIUM TO THE COTTON TEXTILE INDUSTRY

By HENRY P. KENDALL

President, The Kendall Company [1]

DEPRESSIONS in the cotton textile industry have recurred with such insistence that they may be said to have become chronic. They run through a cycle of overproduction; glutted markets, and acceptance of under-cost prices for quantities of distress merchandise, shutdowns, and unemployment. The effects of this cycle are disruptive not only to the some half million individuals and their families directly looking to the industry for support, but to the entire business community, for industry and business today are interdependent to a degree never before realized in economic history. Idle mills cannot sustain large taxation. Development of schools, roads, streets, and public improvements is impeded. Enforced idleness, which follows the piling up of stocks, means curtailment of purchasing which reduces the volume of business of the merchants and manufacturers of all kinds of consumer goods. Values of mill securities are written down.

Production of any kind of goods in excess of consumptive requirements upsets the equilibrium of trade. There are two lines of approach in restoring the equilibrium: increase of consumptive requirements; regulation of production.

---

[1] One of the integrated enterprises in the textile industry, producing gray goods in five Southern mills and controlling the finishing and cutting-up of the gray goods into finished articles of consumption, many of which are trade marked and advertised and sold through the Company's own sales divisions.

Over a twenty-five-year period, from 1899 to 1925, there has been an increased per capita consumption of cotton textiles amounting to approximately seven square yards per capita. Automobile tire fabric accounts for a considerable share of this increase. Other auto trade uses, such as upholstery, top and cover fabrics, and interlinings, account for the balance. Excluding uses connected with automobile manufacturing, therefore, the per capita use of cotton textiles probably has decreased rather than increased in the twenty-five years.

Immediate, needed relief cannot be expected through the sole avenue of increasing consumption, either through development of new uses or through a more intelligent exploitation of markets. It is futile to debate whether the troubles of the industry are due to overproduction or underconsumption, as long as goods are produced in such quantities that they cannot be absorbed into the stream of demand at prices permitting a fair profit. Nothing will be gained by continuing the past practice of playing peek-a-boo with the law of supply and demand.

Whatever will help to develop new uses, to integrate selling with producing, and to exploit markets with every scientific resource, is urgently needed in this diffused industry with its 1600 or so individual units. The history of this first American manufacturing industry is a history of disjointedness. Textile mill owners permitted functions to be parcelled out among various people instead of developing a control which would follow through from raw material to consumer of finished product. Mill agents, commission men, commercial bleaching and finishing plants, brokers, converters—all have grown up. The industry has not progressed in the knowledge and practice of modern management principles. Cotton mills have made any kind of cloth by adding new equipment, instead of developing along single-purpose lines where the greatest economies lie.

The conception of modern merchandising, as requiring constant and alert contact with changing markets, has not been adopted. The Southern cycle of textile development added mills, many of them too small to do direct selling. As other industries were tending toward integration, cotton textiles became more scattered, broken up and diffused. Failures, receiverships, and changes in ownership have not brought relief. Attrition does not seem to work. Bankrupt mills are bought in at receiver's sales for 25 cents or 10 cents on the dollar. The ensuing low-cost competition becomes anything but a constructive element in the situation. Women's clothing changed in style. Rayon and silk became competitors. The war-time demand for cotton goods was so great that every mill could sell its output at a profit, and production accelerated tremendously, especially in the South where labor laws permitted night operation.

These and many other factors are a part of the picture of an opportunistic development which has meant that coordination of supply and demand has come perhaps as far from realization in cotton textiles as in any other American industry. Balancing production more nearly with consumption requires strenuous measures, and calls for a type of cooperation to which the industry is not habituated but which it is coming to recognize as a first essential to restoration of the equilibrium.

The long hours of work in cotton textiles have been one of the main roots of overproduction. In Maine, New Hampshire, Vermont, and to some extent Connecticut and Rhode Island, mills operate 54 hours a week; in North and South Carolina, 55 hours and upward and in other Southern states, 55, 56, and 60 hours. Night running is widespread. In November, 1929, I wrote a letter to President Hoover in which the following proposal was made regarding hours, and the excerpt may be pertinent:

The action (to reduce overproduction) I would suggest would

be to secure by mutual consent an agreement permanently to reduce the working hours in all textile mills to not over fifty; to
pay the same weekly wage for fifty hours that was paid for fifty-
four, fifty-five or sixty, whatever schedule the individual mills
operated on; and in mills that operate day and night to replace
positions left vacant by women workers on the day shift by women
workers from the night shift, and to replace, just as far as possible,
vacancies appearing among women workers on the night shift,
with men.

It might be inopportune at the present time to endeavor to
eliminate night running in cotton mills. It might temporarily
throw people out of work. Perhaps such a move could be arrived
at later. I believe the industry as a whole would benefit from it.

The reduction of hours to a number not over fifty in any one
week would give more leisure and a higher standing of living;
would permanently bring a reduction in output which would offset in part the overproduction now existing, and would raise the
average earnings of operatives, because for some years the industry
has not operated to capacity and the workers have been the
principal sufferers.

The foregoing letter seemed to arouse a great deal of interest and to express the belief of many people within the industry. Since it was written, the industry has adopted a plan to
reduce day running to 55 hours a week and night running to
50 hours. There is at present considerable discussion of elimination entirely of night running. The industry generally
appears more open-minded on the subject of correctives than
has been true in times past.[2]

Cooperative action is difficult to secure in an industry with
hundreds of scattered units, many of them small. Generally
speaking, the resources for doing business in the cotton textile
field have not been massed as has been the case in such indus-

---

[2] Since Mr. Kendall's chapter was written, the Cotton-Textile Institute has taken
action which seems to promise within the near future elimination of women and
minors from the night shift.

tries as steel, and this is a factor to be reckoned with in estimating the possibilities of progressive, cooperative action.

Together with reduction of hours of work for operatives and maintenance of wages—lifting the industry out of the long-hour, low-wage group—other measures are necessary if a more normal balance between production and demand is to be assured. The industry needs more merchandising, more research, more emphasis on creation, more acceptance of the modern, scientific attitude toward business. It needs leadership. It needs strong hands, intelligent hands.

IV

A PLAN FOR ORGANIZING SPECIFIC INDUSTRY

The Woolen and Worsted Piece Goods and Yarn Division of the Wool Industry

By A. D. WHITESIDE

President, The Wool Institute, Inc.

THE potential capacity of the wool industry exceeds current demand by a wide margin. In 1927 the consumption of woolen and worsted fabrics amounted to approximately $656,-000,000, as compared with a maximum manufacturing capacity of $1,750,000,000 at current prices.

Potential production figures for the weaving and spinning divisions of the woolen and worsted piece goods and yarn divisions of the wool industry, furnish a rough measure of excess capacity.

1929

WEAVING DIVISION

Potential Production	Actual Consumption	%
$1,465,000,000	$550,000,000	37.5

SPINNING DIVISION

Potential Production	Actual Consumption	%
232,000,000 pounds	83,109,139 pounds	35.8

While the tendency to produce beyond market requirements inheres in modern industry, excess capacity in its present proportions is a more recent development. The question of methods to be adopted to prevent overproduction is the most important single subject for economic and political consideration in the world today. And until this fact is recognized, no adequate means will be worked out for balancing normal supply and demand. "Balanced Prosperity" will remain a theoretical objective.

PLAN OF ORGANIZATION

Until very recently a haze of mystery has hung over the conditions surrounding the relationship of supply and demand, particularly where world markets have been involved.

Only the largest operators or the particularly astute men in any business had reliable information on which to plan buying for production and operating schedules and, in many instances, even the most successful men worked only on intuitive hunches, which turned out to be right a higher percentage of times than those of the average man in business.

The larger concerns usually dealt in or near the Raw Material Market, and if materials were converted into semi-finished or finished products, the scale of operations was sufficiently broad to keep them in more intimate touch with the sources of supply and the trend of demand—and consequently prices—than was possible for their customers, who were generally smaller operators.

While in those days the relationship between supply and demand was the irrevocable pendulum ultimately determining the price level, the actual economic action of this law could be manipulated and either retarded or expedited by the action of a comparatively few large operators who almost invariably dealt largely in first-hand commodities.

But for the past five or six years or more that mystery has been eliminated and the specific knowledge of the relationship between supply and demand at a given time is an open book, not only to the second- and third-hand users of commodities, but literally even to the man on the street.

This comparatively recent change from the day when rumor and manipulation controlled the price situation to the present time, when the facts relating to Market conditions are available from the point of origin of the Raw Material to the amount of stocks on the retail shelves, has been so sudden that industry as a whole has not been able to readjust its prospectus to cope with this new situation.

It seems evident that industry in general does not grasp the vital significance of the fact that this common knowledge of true conditions calls for an entire reversal in the attitude of business men toward each other.

In the past, business men followed the policy of isolation and individualism to guard secrets which they thought gave them a trading advantage over their competitors.

Now that every rational business man knows that mysteries, which give one an advantage over another, no longer exist, closer and closer relationship between business men must be established if the disastrous results of the lack of organization in industry are to be eradicated.

One point cannot be too emphatically stressed.

That is—the fact that institutes have been formed and that the motions of coordination have been gone through by many industries, without tangible results, does not in any way signify that the industries involved have been actually organized in any sense of the word.

Institutes so far have been floundering in an endeavor to find the practical methods which will conclusively yield satisfactory results.

Many institutes are seriously handicapped because their first efforts, which were along somewhat theoretical lines, did not work out satisfactorily, and those that participated in these activities have now condemned coordination because the first feeble or misdirected efforts did not bring about the anticipated results.

The organized activities which can be carried out and which will inevitably result to the very great advantage of every participating business unit and to the very decided benefit of the industry as a whole are as follows:

STATISTICS OF PRODUCTION, BILLINGS, AND STOCKS WEEKLY OR MONTHLY

I

Under existing conditions, when demand constantly fluctuates, statistics are absolutely essential if goods are to be properly marketed at a fair price. Absolutely accurate data giving each seller assurance of his exact position in the industry, which cannot be obtained in any other way, is furnished through the simple means of having each producer file the figures mentioned.

For instance, if any given group of producers marketed 12,000,-000 units in 1929, on a basis of 1,000,000 units a month, one unit might have done 5 per cent of the total volume of business, which would have been 600,000 units for that year.

If for the seven months ending August 1st the total volume of business done by all producers were 25 per cent below the 1929 level and this one unit which did 5 per cent of the total last year still did 5 per cent of the depreciated total up to August 1st this year, it might well be content with having maintained its relative position in the industry.

If this unit had increased its percentage of the total to 7½ per cent, there might be an incentive to slightly increase the price of its product.

If its percentage of the total had declined to 3½ per cent up to August 1st, it could know that the reason for that decline might be attributed to one or more of the following causes:

> 1st—Its price level might be too high in comparison with the competitive market.

2nd—Its goods might not have been up to competitive standards or properly styled.

3rd—Its sales organization might not be exerting its maximum effort.

4th—The production service might have been inadequate.

At any rate, each unit participating in filing Statistics would be in a position to know the facts or go about finding the facts each month regarding their own position in relationship to that of the industry.

The fundamental causes for falling behind in a highly competitive market are (1) the price level, (2) wrong styling or a deficient product.

The total picture each month of the collective stocks on hand shows immediately whether the manufactured goods unsold were a menace to the price level or not for if accurately known the figures act as a self-regulating barometer.

II

The second group of organization activities that is practical and essential to the welfare of an industry is that which is fundamental in determining the price level, of which the correctness is proved by the concrete knowledge of the relative position of the individual unit as shown through activity Number I.

This second activity is divided into two parts.

If the relative position is not maintained and prices are lowered to increase sales, the individual unit must be in a position to know that the determined cost in figuring the selling price, particularly when the margin of profit is low, as in most instances under existing conditions, is correctly figured. So uniform methods of figuring cost and comparisons of the costs of different products made by the same producers must be figured on a basis of equivalent units and according to a uniform cost method.

If the styling of the product is found to be the kink in maintaining the relative position of the producer, a style service, adequate to guide the industry in the proper channel of the trends in evidence is of material value, and usually eliminates the temptation to directly copy competing styles at a lower price.

III

With these fundamentals worked out and carried out, it readily follows that the self-government of the industry must have the physical mechanism with which to determine and administer the policies of the industry as a whole.

This is done by scheduled meetings of those making related products. At these meetings policies are discussed and presented to the industry for its consideration. Then to prevent misunderstandings and to settle contentious trade practices, rulings must be decided upon and accepted by the industry in general.

With a code of practice as a basis to govern controversies arising between units within the industry, a method of dealing with controversial subjects between the industry and its markets should be arranged by arbitration agreement.

As a final step in the refinement of organization work, no industry should fail to set up a proper research division, not only to study the most efficient methods of production, but to give extensive and broad consideration to the development of markets and new utilities for the products produced.

Industries that are seriously carrying out a program of this nature will, without question, be rewarded by adequate profits and very great contentment to the individuals involved.

Without organization of this nature, or of somewhat similar nature, either modified or elaborated, men in business today cannot seriously have a reasonable expectation that the constant menace of overproduction and the resulting suffering has been overcome.

When these steps are carried out and the individual units making up industry in this country today realize their absolute necessity and their dominating importance in regulating supply and demand, industry will come into its own on a scientific, economic basis which has so far never been attained.

In reviewing the conditions that have always existed, and as far as can be foreseen, always will exist, it seems obvious that overproduction as a menace can only be eliminated through the coordination of industry in first obtaining the data required on which to base its operation, and secondly, to set up the mechanism to educate the individual organizations in the industry to realize the meaning of the facts when available.

V

OVERPRODUCTION IN THE SILK INDUSTRY—ITS CAUSE, EFFECT AND CURE

By THOMAS B. HILL
President, The Silk Association of America, Inc.

THE great increase in women office-workers and changes in the mode of living, especially in the use of closed automobiles, brought about in the years during and immediately after the World War a demand for lighter weight clothes and those which would stand up in appearance throughout the day. Silk dresses apparently fulfilled these requirements and there was a tremendous call for silk fabrics of all kinds to the exclusion of other fabrics. It was during these years that silk manufacturers found themselves in the same position as many other groups that were bending all their energies to meeting demand by improved methods and machinery, increased plants, multiple shifts, and all the other factors utilized in speeding up production of this type of merchandise. This expansion was not only of interest to the silk trade itself, but affected the economic life of the small towns and cities of the Eastern states. Mills were started in hundreds of small villages, throughout the state of Pennsylvania, particularly, and through the New England states. It was comparatively easy to open these plants and put in new machinery, as a silk mill does not require any tremendous investment in equipment. Many of the manufacturers who started in business had had no previous experience in administration. Some of them were skilled workmen and nothing more. Others were financiers who knew

34

nothing about the silk trade or textiles in any form. Still others had been small business men, who saw in the mushroom growth of the silk trade an easy opportunity to make money.

Ownership of the industry rested, consequently, on the shoulders of men who were intent on production rather than distribution, so that today, when we find the silk industry in a position where supply exceeds demand, there is need for far-sighted and able merchandisers. The greatest percentage of profit at the present time in the silk business comes not necessarily from the most efficient mills, the best producers, but rather from the people who know merchandising and who have learned that they cannot make money on ability to produce alone, but only on production of merchandise which can be sold.

Even more serious, however, than the superfluity of equipment and machines has been the style element. Silk has always been considered the leader of the textiles in style, and in former years the business was sufficiently specialized to permit of fairly wide latitude in the creation of styles and in the assumption of style risk. Now that the industry is on a mass-production basis, judgment as to style must be that much keener, as otherwise the consequences of poor judgment in anticipating fashion demand represents one of the costly losses to the industry. This can be demonstrated by a study of inventories of the individual silk merchants. It will, no doubt, be found that in some types of merchandise demand is ahead of supply, but on the contrary, that the same merchant may have on his shelves an alarming liability in large stocks of unwanted goods. This usually represents poor planning or understanding of the style element. It is this situation which makes especially difficult the solution of the overproduction problem in the silk industry. Manufacturers have done many things to cut the cost of production, but these measures have brought disappointment to many firms because the saving on production cost does not offset the losses on stocks of silk fabrics which could not be disposed of except at sacrifice prices. It is a situation that demands closest study from the broadest viewpoint. The owners of silk plants must stand to one side and view their own business from a stranger's outlook. Particularly is this true in the style problem. Probably other industries, classified as fashion industries, find themselves in the same predicament. What will be in demand and how long will it continue? It is difficult to make such forecasts, but a great deal more can be done than has been done in the past by a closer study of sales.

It has been found, for instance, in the silk industry, that fashion enters not only into types of construction and patterns but even into color. It may be, for example, that a deep plum color will be called for and a premium paid for securing it. It has frequently been the case that in such a situation, piece after piece is dyed into plum color which, by the time the goods is ready for sale, finds the demand past. This material then goes with other dead merchandise on the manufacturer's shelves. Another example of style and its effect on overproduction or production of what is not wanted is that of the Jacquard loom. Years ago silk fabrics with a woven figure were extremely popular. Today they are almost unknown except for very few short-lived novelties. Many firms, however, are equipped with a number of these looms. If there is the slightest indication that figured silks are wanted, the manufacturer who believes he saves expenses by keeping his machinery running will immediately start turning out quantities of a fabric which probably in a week or so will be a dead issue. The same problem arose some years ago in the changing from plain woven fabrics to the crepe fabrics. Manufacturers who had many dollars tied up in looms for the weaving of taffetas and similar fabrics found themselves with so many frozen assets on their hands. Unfortuniately, some of the firms, by not watching carefully the trend of demand on the part of the public, continued making taffetas, despite the fact that at one point a year or so ago, there were indications that the demand for taffetas could be entirely supplied by the current production and stock of just one of the firms. This instinct of the producer to use his machinery and keep his people steadily employed is a liability when that same manufacturer does not make a careful analysis of his markets and an even more careful study of how to apply mass production to a style product. Change in style is one of the chief problems of the producer with large responsibilities in producing capacity.

In the silk trade another problem has been the change in type of demand during the past ten years. Formerly, the manufacturer's trade was principally in the wholesale and retail houses for advance orders of large quantities, and he could plan his production accordingly. In the last decade, however, there has arisen the gigantic ready-to-wear trade, popularly known as the "cutting-up" industry. This group of fabric buyers is almost exclusively centered in New York, and the fabric manufacturer quickly found that these buyers wanted immediate service and did not plan their buying as the wholesale and retail trade had in previous years. This meant that the manufacturer must learn to carry stocks of merchandise in wanted colors and patterns; he must assume a greater risk than ever in carrying unwanted silks. He must increase his cost of doing business because his orders now were not for a hundred full ·pieces of sixty yards each for delivery by freight or express some months or weeks later, but rather for small quantities to be delivered at once. The tremendously increased demand coming from this new element in buying fabrics created an abnormally optimistic attitude on the part of many producers of silks. In addition to selling finished piece goods direct, they found also a new class of buyer in numerous salesmen formerly in the employ of silk houses, who were going into business independently as so-called "jobbers." These people developed into a class now known as "converters," and represent those who buy woven fabrics unfinished, or what is termed "raw goods." The apparent lack of risk in making up raw goods without the necessity of finishing it also resulted in overproduction. Such stocks, of course, are dangerous only through quantity rather than type as previously discussed. But these elements, style risk, change in distribution channels and change in types of fabrics, have all brought about the present chaotic condition existing in the industry.

Silk manufacturers, however, are now beginning to make constructive recommendations for the betterment of conditions. There are, of course, difficulties involved in making radical changes in production, when millions of dollars are invested in plant equipment and when whole towns depend upon one mill for bread and butter. But in order to create a normal condition that will insure a more reliable basis of operation, manufacturers feel that they must make a closer study of what is being sold and to what extent. Then must come an application of that study to their inventories. An analysis of past records has indicated that the nearest approach to control of inventories through sales is to take as a basis a peak ratio of monthly inventories not exceeding two and one-half times the average monthly sales. This figure, it is believed, will allow ample latitude for service to the buyer. Demonstrations of this principle are now being given to the silk trade through meetings of the Silk Association of America. Through the individual effort of manufacturers of silk fabrics, it is hoped that it will be possible to solve what is considered to be the most serious problem ever confronting the trade since the days when it was first established in this country in the middle of the nineteenth century.

The most promising aspect is the fact that the industry has a product which is used almost to the exclusion of other members of the textile family, one which meets the demands of present-day life and which for centuries has been considered the most desirable of all apparel fabrics. On the other hand, the industry must find an answer to the problem of adjustment of mass production to a product controlled by style. A closer study, however, of their current markets, and an application of that information to their products, will, it is believed, point the way for the constructively thinking silk manufacturer and distributor.

VI

THE RAYON INDUSTRY

By JOHN E. BASSILL
Vice-President, Tubize Chatillon Corporation

A. SIZE AND IMPORTANCE OF THE INDUSTRY

ALTHOUGH rayon was first invented in 1884, it was really not until after the World War that the industry began to expand rapidly to its present size. The position of rayon in the world's textile industry is shown in the following table as a percentage of the total poundage production. It will be noted that rayon is the only one of the four major fibers to show a constantly increasing standing during the years shown.

TABLE I

PER CENT OF WORLD PRODUCTION

	Cotton	Wool	Silk	Rayon
1913	81.60	17.90	0.35	0.15
1922	76.62	22.15	0.57	0.66
1925	81.06	17.33	0.51	1.10
1926	81.09	17.18	0.55	1.18
1927	76.33	21.27	0.66	1.74
1928	76.35	20.84	0.62	2.19
1929	76.54	20.41	0.64	2.41

Table II below shows the best available estimates of world production during 1913 in recent years.

TABLE II

RAYON PRODUCTION BY COUNTRIES

(Millions of Pounds)

Country	1913	1922	1924	1926	1927	1928	1929
United States.......	1.6	24.4	38.7	62.6	75.5	97.9	122.1
Italy...............	......	6.3	18.5	35.0	36.0	47.0	59.0
Great Britain.......	11.5	15.3	23.9	25.5	39.0	52.0	52.7
Germany...........	7.8	12.6	23.7	26.0	31.0	41.0	45.0
France.............	3.1	6.3	12.3	17.5	21.0	30.0	37.0
Holland............	......	2.5	3.4	13.5	16.5	16.5	20.0
Japan..............	......	0.2	1.2	5.5	8.0	12.0	18.0
Belgium............	3.0	6.3	8.9	13.1	13.5	15.0	15.0
Switzerland........	0.3	1.9	4.0	8.0	10.0	12.0	12.2
All Others..........	1.5	5.1	6.6	12.4	16.7	21.2	25.0
World total.......	28.8	80.9	141.2	219.1	267.2	344.6	406.0

It will be noted that the United States is now the largest world producer of rayon, making 30 per cent of the total world production in 1929. Rapid strides in rayon production have been made especially by Italy and Japan in recent years, while countries which were early producers of rayon, such as Holland and Belgium, have fallen behind relatively.

Turning to the American rayon market, it may be seen in Table III below that the United States produces about 88 per cent of all the rayon consumed in this country and imports only about 12 per cent, rayon exports from this country being negligible. Principally due to price cuts in 1930, the amount of rayon imported to this country has dropped appreciably and will probably amount to only 6 per cent or less of the total domestic consumption in 1930.

Although United States consumption of rayon in 1930 promises only to equal the 1929 consumption, it is undoubtedly true that 1930 will prove to be but a pause in the upward

TABLE III

ANNUAL RAYON DATA FOR UNITED STATES

	Thousands of Pounds			Per Cent	
	Produced In U. S.*	Imported	U. S. Consumption*	Produced in U. S.	Imported
1913............	1,567	2,305	3,872	40.4	59.6
1922............	24,434	2,088	26,522	92.1	7.9
1923............	36,153	3,906	38,429	89.8	10.2
1924............	39,092	1,712	40,804	95.8	4.2
1925............	51,792	7,002	58,794	89.1	11.9
1926............	63,648	10,063	66,711	86.3	13.7
1927............	75,522	16,236	101,000	82.3	17.7
1928............	97,901	12,747	110,000	88.5	11.5
1929............	122,066	15,903	135,000	88.5	11.5
1930*...........	125,000	8,000	133,000	94.0	6.0

* Estimated.

swing of rayon consumption. Given reasonable price stability, the consumptive demand for rayon has by no means begun to reach the saturation point, nor is there any evidence pointing to a tapering off of the rapid growth of the industry in recent years.

In 1922, knit goods (principally knit outerwear) and hosiery were the two fields which consumed the largest percentage of rayon in the United States. During 1929, however, the underwear industry was the largest user followed by cotton weavers and hosiery manufacturers. The percentage of rayon used in various industries by years from 1922 to 1929 is shown in Table IV following.

New uses of rayon are being discovered constantly and it is quite possible that the above ratios will be considerably altered in the next few years. For example, rayon is becoming more successful in the full-fashioned hosiery industry; the

TABLE IV

PERCENTAGE OF RAYON USED IN VARIOUS INDUSTRIES
(United States)

	1922	1923	1924	1925	1926	1927	1928	1929
Underwear manufacturers.....	4	5	11	13	24	28	32	32
Cotton weavers...............	10	11	15	26	21	24	21	21
Hosiery manufacturers........	24	22	23	28	25	21	18	19
Silk weavers.................	11	15	18	16	14	14	14	13
Braids......................	11	10	8	4	1	2	5	5
Knit goods..................	26	25	14	5	3	4	4	4
Wool manufacturers...........	1	1	1	1	1	1	1	1
Miscellaneous...............	13	4	10	7	11	6	5	5
Total...................	100	100	100	100	100	100	100	100

men's underwear field is one that has great possibilities for the use of rayon; and coat and suit linings of rayon have been meeting with unusual success recently, only to mention a few of the newer developments.

B. SOME OF THE ECONOMIC FACTORS INVOLVED

If we define the utility of a good as its ability to satisfy human wants, and if we define production as the agency which supplies form, time, or place utility to any form of economic wealth, we may say that the rayon industry essentially consists of adding form utility to the raw materials of the industry in such a way as to make rayon. The final cost of rayon to weavers or knitters is composed of the five general sub-heads of the raw material cost, the operating expense, the overhead of plant and machinery, the selling expense, and the profit. Large-scale operation in the rayon industry, under capable management, undoubtedly results in a lowering of each and every one of these expense items. First, we must conclude, then, that the rayon industry best consists of large-scale operating units and does not lend itself to small unit operation.

The second point to be noted in connection with the rayon industry is the factor of substitution. The invention of rayon by Count de Chardonnet in 1884 was activated by his desire to produce a fiber which would resemble silk. From that time until about 1923, this man-made fiber was called artificial silk because it was intended to be substituted for silk. Then the textile industry began to realize that this newest-of-the-fibers had peculiar properties of its own which should allow it to stand on its own merits and not be merely something "practically as good as" something else. From that time on, the generic name of the fiber became rayon and it came to compete not only with silk but also with cotton, and, to a less extent, with wool. Thus, although silk undoubtedly continues to be the greatest competitor of rayon, the latter fiber has made gradually increasing inroads on the fields formerly held by cotton (particularly mercerized cotton) and, in some cases, into the wool industry. The factor of substitution, then, is a most important one in the textile industry and is of especial importance to the rayon branch of that industry.

Rayon is a man-machine-made fiber and its production may be controlled even from day to day. Cotton, silk, and wool, on the other hand, may be called the natural fibers because their growth or production is determined more by natural forces than by man-made forces. Thus, during any one crop year, the total cotton produced depends not only on the acreage planted and the fertilizer used as determined by man, but also on the weather, the boll-weevil, and other pests, etc., which are relatively beyond human control. Further, the production of rayon is centered in the hands of relatively very few producers as compared with the thousands of decentralized producers of cotton, silk, or wool. Rayon production, then, is susceptible to the closest production control of any of the major textile fibers.

This brings us to the problem of overproduction. In the case of most economic goods during periods of normal business activity and especially in the case of substitutive, necessary goods such as textiles, lower prices tend to increase the consumptive demand for the article. All other factors remaining constant, lower prices will stimulate the demand for goods under normal business conditions, although this principle may have no effect during periods of business depression. At any given price for a certain article, there will be a fairly definite volume of demand for that article largely based on the relative prices of other competing or substitutive goods. The profit problem of any industry, therefore, becomes a matter of adjusting production to demand at the optimum price, that price at which the most goods are sold at the greatest net profit to the producer.

The so-called business cycles, or, from the viewpoint of producers, the rhythmic periods of alternate overproduction and underproduction, are largely caused by their failure to regulate their production to demand. Manufacturers generally have rightly focused their attention on profits and when they see the prices of their product rising, they are immediately stimulated to produce more in an effort to increase their profits. The only difficulty with this procedure is that they not only produce too much, but also the so-called marginal producers are drawn into production to swell the total output. The result is obvious; prices fall not because of reduced demand but rather because of increased supply. Profits likewise fall, the marginal producers drop out of production, and hard times come. The goose that laid the golden eggs of high profits is destroyed principally because of a short-sighted policy. Even then the larger producers shut their eyes to the need for curtailed production in order to offset the previous orgy of activity and the situation becomes worse. Finally, in desperation, they realize the necessity of curtailing their operations and the plants are reduced to low rates of activity. Follows a period of depression, mental as well as economic, but eventually demand catches up with the overproduced supply, prices strengthen and then rise, and the whole cycle begins over again.

Summing up the foregoing discussion, the following points may be noted. (1) The rayon industry is one in which large-scale unit operation is necessary. (2) Rayon is in a competitive and substitutive field where it may replace other fibers, or, vice versa, may be replaced by them. (3) Because of this fact the price of rayon relative to the prices of the other fibers is most important. (4) The price of rayon is not the leading determinant in the general level of textile prices; that is, rayon prices follow the prices of other textiles rather than determine them because, (5) the production of rayon is much more subject to control than is the production of any of the other major textile fibers. (6) Overproduction is a relative term and must be so used. This point is considered further in the next section.

C. THE PROBLEM OF OVERPRODUCTION

Focusing attention on the rayon industry, it is a well-known fact that the sales of rayon producers and of the industry as a whole contain the three basic elements of long time or secular growth, seasonal variation, and cyclical variation or periods of business advance and recession. The growth of rayon consumption, or its secular trend, has been discussed in the first section of this article. The line of secular growth may be called the 100 per cent line or the average performance which may be expected in any year, say from one to five years in advance. It is believed that this growth will continue at its old rate for several more years before beginning to flatten off and finally become fairly stable. This factor is not one that is essentially concerned in the problem of overproduction in the rayon industry as it exists today.

The second element, that of seasonal variation, refers to the fact that at certain times of the year, sales are usually larger than they are at other times of the year. Thus, in the rayon industry, producers' sales during the summer and winter months are normally smaller than they are during the spring and fall months. This condition is caused by the fact that, as Professor Paul Douglas has well put it, "styles in textiles are as perishable as vegetables"; for weavers and knitters, wholesalers and retailers must fill their orders at those times of the year when the demands of new season buying of styled goods are made. This factor is beyond the control of rayon producers, and because it is a temporary as well as a periodic phenomenon, it results in relatively small and easily retrievable amounts of overproduction.

If the secular growth line is called 100 per cent or normal, and if seasonal variation is eliminated from the sales by statistical methods, the residual series of data will show the cyclical variation of sales plus a small amount of sporadic fluctuation. It is this cyclical variation which is most important from the standpoint of overproduction.

The sequences of these business cycles, or alternate periods of business advance and recession, have already been discussed in the previous section. The problem of their solution resolves itself into two questions: (1) "What can be done by rayon producers so as to alleviate these cycles in their business, dispose of the problem of overproduction, and give some stability to profits?" and (2) "What may other business agencies do to attain this same end?"

In answer to the first question, the following suggestions are made:

1. The rayon industry as a whole should cooperate to furnish its members, as well as others who are interested, complete and comprehensive figures on the amount of rayon produced, sold, and held in stock.

2. Producers should analyze their sales and the sales of the industry so as to determine the extent and direction of a cyclical variation in sales. Then when this cycle begins to turn down, production should be restricted immediately and proportionally to the extent of the downcoming. In this connection, it is interesting to note that the cycle of rayon sales has rather closely followed the cycle of general textile activity as reported monthly by the Federal Reserve Board.

3. Because rayon yarn sales by producers do follow the cycles of general textile production, it is apparent that the cycle of rayon yarn sales is determined principally by rayon users and not by rayon producers. Therefore, although rayon producers may *anticipate* cyclical periods in their sales and may adjust their productive activity to their sales so as to avoid overproduction, nevertheless they are in no position to *alleviate* the existing sales cycles inasmuch as the needs of the knitting and weaving trades must be filled. This statement is not to be construed as "passing the buck" to the knitting and weaving sections of the textile industry for these sections, in turn, must also fill the needs of their customers. In short, the blame for overproduction in the rayon or any other industry can seldom be laid at the door of any one industry. We must look to more basic causes for the general, and therefore the specific, causes of overproduction in industry.

This brings us to the second main question above, namely, "What may other business agencies do to attain stability in production?"

1. Without attempting to answer this question with any semblance of completeness, it is believed that one of the most

efficacious of such agencies is the Federal Reserve Board. The potential power of the Board in the money market through its open-market operations, as well as the discount rate, make it the greatest single agency in the money market. And the money market is undoubtedly the most important single determinant of business activity in the long run. Of course, there would be many adverse criticisms of the Board were it to tighten credit when business *begins* to go above normal—cries of "killing business," "inviting depression," etc. But a slight depression is, after all, much more desirable than a severe one such as most businesses, and the textile industry in particular, have been experiencing during 1930.

The question which will always be asked, in the determination of Federal Reserve policy, is "What is normal?" It is believed that the answer to this question can be satisfactorily determined once there is a specific demand for a more even keel in business.

2. A second but probably less important factor which could be changed so as to help iron out the business cycle is the group of anti-trust laws. Briefly, this series of laws prohibits all combinations "in restraint of trade." Inasmuch as no definition of just what constitutes restraint of trade has ever been given, each case of supposed transgression has to be judged on its own merits. It is interesting to note that the Webb-Pomerene Act of 1919 specifically allows combinations of all sorts *for export purposes,* but the old basic Sherman and Clayton Acts still prohibit such domestic combinations. Thus it would appear that what is good for the goose is not good for the gander. We do not advocate great monopolistic combines which would stifle the small producer; but we do believe that some sort of combination for the purpose of controlling production, and, therefore, the business cycle, should be allowed and should be encouraged in domestic industries. Such cooperatives are now allowed under the Federal Farm Act and public utilities have

operated rather satisfactorily as monopolies under government supervision for over forty years.   It is only reasonable to believe, therefore, that some plan could also be worked out for business groups so that they could attempt to control overproduction both individually and collectively.

In conclusion, it would seem that there must be an extensive, popular, and consistent demand for business stability before the problem of overproduction in industry can be intelligently approached and solved.   Such a demand is now present in all branches of business from capital to labor.   It is interesting to note, however, that this desire is commonly expressed only during such periods of extreme depression as are now being witnessed; during periods of normal business or in times of so-called prosperity, the cry is no longer heard. Depressed business today with its cries of stabilization will be the prosperous business of tomorrow with its smug equanimity and a demeanor oblivious to the dangers besetting it on next day.   The chief answer to overproduction is collective business and political foresight assisted by the dissemination and intelligent interpretation of trade statistics and information.

VII

OVERPRODUCTION IN AGRICULTURE

By DR. O. E. BAKER

Senior Agricultural Economist, United States Department of Agriculture

THE surplus continues to be the great problem in American agriculture. Despite an increase in the nation's population of about 15 million in the decade since the war, and with practically no increase in the acreage of crop land and practically no decrease in the aggregate exports of farm products, the farmers of the nation continue to produce more than they can sell at a profit. Evidently there has been a large increase in production per acre, yet acre yields of the crops have increased only slightly, if at all. Let us seek the causes of this strange situation, even though the cure may not be clear.

THE CAUSES OF THE SURPLUS

Most, if not all, of the causes can be traced to the application of scientific technique to agriculture, and these applications are myriad in number. However, several of these advances in technique are of such outstanding importance that it will be helpful in understanding the situation to note them particularly:

1. The introduction and increasing use of the automobile and tractor have permitted a reduction of over 7,000,000 horses and mules since the war, and thereby released between 20,000,-000 and 25,000,000 acres of crops, which are now used mostly to feed meat and milk animals and to grow cotton. As about

200,000,000 acres were used for these purposes in 1919, it appears that this crop land released by the decline in horses and mules has provided an increase of about 10 per cent in the decade in the acreage available for the production of meat, milk and cotton. This is an increase two-thirds as great as the increase in the nation's population.

2. There has been a notable increase in the production of meat and milk per unit of feed consumed. This is owing, first, to decreased production of pork and beef in the South and increased production in the North and West, where the animals, in general, are of better stock and more efficient in transforming feed into food. There are, for instance, scarcely more than half as many hogs south of the Ohio and Potomac rivers as there were ten years ago. On the other hand, there are 20 to 100 per cent more hogs in the states from Minnesota and Iowa to Kansas and westward, excluding the Pacific coast. There has been a corresponding shift in corn acreage and the yield per acre of corn is about twice as high in Iowa and Minnesota as in the South. Undoubtedly, the large amount of feed released by the decline in horses and mules in the North and West has been an important cause of this increasing concentration of meat and milk production in the West North Central States.

A second group of causes of this increasing production of meat and milk per unit of feed consumed are improvements in farm practices. The cow-testing associations and other agencies have promoted the selection of the larger-producing cows and the slaughter of the poorer cows. There has been little increase in the number of cows during the past decade, but the production of milk has increased, apparently, about 30 per cent. Feed eaten by the cows has increased, apparently, only 20 to 25 per cent. Likewise, there are fewer hogs on farms than a decade ago, but the production of pork and lard is about 20 per cent greater. Better sanitation has resulted in saving almost one more pig per litter, on the average, and the feed that the dead pig had eaten is now saved. Also more legumes and minerals are being used and more growth is obtained on the same amount of feed. Beef cattle and sheep are being slaughtered at an earlier age, and young animals make more gain on the same amount of feed than old animals.

The significance of this increasing production of meat and milk per unit of feed consumed, becomes evident when it is realized that 70 per cent of the crop land and all of the pasture is used to feed farm animals. Over 80 per cent of the sustenance yielded by the soil each year in the United States is eaten by farm animals. It is probable that the increased efficiency of the nation's live stock in transforming feed into food is as important a factor as the tractor and automobile in accounting for the great increase in agricultural production since the war.

3. Less important, yet a significant factor, has been the shift from the less productive crops per acre to the more productive; particularly from corn toward cotton in the South, a crop which is worth much more per acre, from wheat toward corn in the North, and from grain and hay toward fruit and vegetables in several areas, notably in California.

4. Likewise there has been a shift from beef cattle toward dairy cattle, hogs, and chickens, which produce much more food than beef cattle per unit of feed consumed. The American people consume, on the average, about 1,400,000 calories of food a year, and to produce this number of calories per capita requires only about ⅓ of an acre of sugar beets or sugar cane, ¾ of an acre of corn or potatoes, 1½ acres of wheat or tomatoes, 2½ acres of grain, hay and silage fed to dairy cows, 3 acres of corn and other products fed to hogs, but about 11 acres of grain and hay fed to beef cattle, besides several acres of pasture. A diet in which the protein and fats are supplied largely by pork, lard, and milk requires much less land than

one in which these essentials are supplied by beef, and still less land is required when the diet consists largely of the cereals and other plant foodstuffs. It requires about two acres of crops to feed the average American, only about one acre to feed a German, ½ acre to feed a Chinese, and ¼ acre to feed a Japanese. In Germany and Japan, however, part of this difference is due to higher acre yields of the crops than in the United States.

WILL THE CAUSES CONTINUE?

Two of these four factors that have promoted the rapid increase of agricultural production since the war seem likely to persist for several years. There are less than half enough colts being raised to replace the horses and mules that die or become incapacitated yearly, consequently the replacement of horses by tractors appears inevitable for several years at least. Moreover, the use of the combine in association with the tractor seems likely to result in a continued expansion of grain production into the semi-arid areas of the West. The improvements in farm practice, particularly those that have contributed to greater production of meat and milk per unit of feed consumed, probably will continue for many years. In addition, it is becoming evident that even at present prices of farm products, it would pay to use more fertilizer, and if prices of farm products should become higher, the use of fertilizers would be greatly encouraged.

Moreover, it is probable that new factors tending to increase agricultural production will rise to importance in the future as they have in the past. Every discovery in agricultural chemistry or biology, every invention in the field of agricultural machinery or the utilization of waste products, every improvement in agricultural practice tends to increase production; and the prospect is that with the Federal Department of Agriculture and 48 State Experiment Stations, besides all the private industries serving the farmers of the United States, constantly pursuing research for the promotion of agriculture, production will increase as rapidly in the future as in the past, provided the prices of farm products resume pre-war trends. The point of diminishing returns is not fixed, but recedes with every improvement in agricultural technique.

But if prices of the major farm products should fall, or perhaps if they should remain stationary, which seems not unlikely, as production in the world as a whole, at least of the cereals, is increasing more rapidly than population, it may develop that aggregate agricultural production in the United States will not advance as rapidly as population during the next decade or more. Although the present generation of farmers will continue to farm for a much smaller compensation than that received by any other occupational group, because there is no alternative employment for old farmers and little other for farmers of middle age, the farmer's children are migrating to the cities so rapidly that the total farm population has decreased ten per cent in the last ten years. This migration may, before long, stabilize production.

This hopeful outlook, however, is clouded by the fact that the nation is entering an era of diminishing increase of population, with the prospect of a stationary, possibly declining, population a few decades hence.

THE POPULATION PROSPECT

The birth rate in the United States is decreasing so rapidly that despite the increasing population the total number of children born annually is now declining, according to the Census. Although the rural birth rate is higher than the urban, the decline is occurring at about the same rate in rural as in urban territory. This decreasing number of children is reflected in the enrollment in the primary grades of the public schools. The number of children in the first grade has been decreasing since 1918, except for a stationary condition from 1922 to 1924 and a rise in 1927, which reflected the transitory increase of births in 1921. This decrease in children in the first grade may be owing in part to greater effort to prevent stagnation in this grade. However, the number of children in the second grade of the public schools has been declining since 1922, and in the third grade since 1924. The more rapid decrease in the birth rate since 1924 is not yet reflected in the school enrollment figures.

It is clear that a decreasing number of children will mean a decreasing population a generation hence, unless the decrease be balanced by immigration, or the duration of life increases. The net immigration at present averages about 250,000 a year, whereas the decrease in number of births averages about 50,000 a year. Five years hence, therefore, if the present downward trend in births continues, and the immigration laws are not altered, the flow of people, so to speak, into the nation, including immigrants, will be no larger than the number of births today. The number of births today is only sufficient to maintain a stationary population of about 140,000,000, having the present average age at death of 59 years. Although this average age at death may increase slightly, it appears unlikely that the United States will ever have over 160,000,000 people, unless the number of births or of immigrants increases. This is a third greater than the population at present.

The slackening in population growth will occur very slowly. The 1930 Census will reveal, probably, a population of about 122,000,000, which would give an increase of over 15,000,000 since 1920. This will be a larger increase than has occurred during any decade in the past, except 1900–1910. In the decade 1930–1940 the increase in population may be not much over 11,000,000, and from 1940 to 1950 it will be still less. It is unlikely this stationary condition will be reached before 1960, and whether the population will afterward decline is dependent not only on the birth rate but also on immigration policy.

THE AGRICULTURAL SIGNIFICANCE OF THE POPULATION PROSPECT

A stationary population in the United States would have serious consequences for the American farmer, whose production has increased probably over 50 per cent in the last thirty years and over 20 per cent in the last ten years, and which might double if prices of farm products should rise to and remain at the war-time peak. A decreasing population would be a calamity, if present conditions of production persisted and larger markets were not found abroad. Farm land values doubtless would decline almost everywhere, farms would be abandoned more extensively than at present, taxes on the remaining land in the less fertile farming areas would rise and force the abandonment of still more farms, the maintenance of schools and roads would become increasingly difficult in these localities, the young people would flock from the farms to the cities even more rapidly than they are doing today, and forest or brush would creep down the mountains and slowly occupy many of the valleys—in brief, the present tendency to concentrate production on the more fertile or favorably located land would be accentuated.

Moreover, the rapid movement of many young people from the farms to the cities would tend to aggravate the population trend, because urban birth rates are, and doubtless will remain, lower than rural birth rates. One of the causes of the rapid decline in the birth rate since the war has been the greater movement of young people from farm to city than ever before, and the decreasing proportion which the farm population constitutes of the nation's population.

SUGGESTIONS THAT HAVE BEEN MADE TO MEET THE SITUATION

Population during the last ten years has increased about 1.4 per cent a year, but the increase is diminishing; agricultural production during the last decade has increased on the average over 2 per cent a year. Faced with the prospect of continued pressure of production on population, several things have been suggested to improve the outlook. Let us consider the feasibility of these suggestions with reference to the present agricultural situation.

1. It has been suggested that an educational campaign might be inaugurated for the purpose of increasing the birth rate. But as it costs at least an eighth of the average man's salary to care for and educate a child, it is obvious that to have three children, which is the average number per fertile family required to maintain even a stationary population, would mean a lower standard of living than if only one or two children were born. A lower standard of living is one of the things which people are most reluctant to accept.

A man's earning power does not increase in proportion to the number of his children, indeed, if there be no children it is often possible for the wife to work and augment the income. Undoubtedly, our system of urban economic individualism is approaching a crucial test, and it may develop that owing to increasing knowledge of birth control and decreasing respect for religious beliefs, some modification of the present system will soon be indicated. Whether government aid in the care of children, such as has already been extended in provision for free education, will be effective only the future can reveal. Certainly this means of improving the agricultural situation appears unlikely to be effective for the present.

2. It has been suggested that the immigration quota might be increased. Although such a raising of the quota probably

would result in increased immigration from most countries, owing to the higher wages in the United States than elsewhere, it might not obtain sufficient immigration twenty or thirty years hence from Northern Europe to balance the upward tendency in agricultural production in the United States, because by that time population in Northern Europe is likely to be stationary or declining.[1] Should it become necessary to depend in part on Southern Europe or Asia for immigration, a modification of the immigration law very likely would meet not only with opposition from organized labor but also from many people interested in maintaining a Teutonic majority in the United States. This means of improving the agricultural situation, therefore may be dismissed from further consideration.

3. If no way of increasing population should prove feasible, it might be possible to increase consumption of agricultural products per person. This object could be achieved by inducing the people to eat less cereal foods and more meat, especially beef. But such a shift has already taken place, and the recent decline in beef consumption suggests that consumption of meat is not likely to increase greatly in the near future. The consumption of meat in the United States is high compared with other countries, and the consumption of cereal foods is low. The consumption per person of cereal foods in the five-year period, 1914–1918, was about 310 pounds, whereas a decade later, during the years 1924–1928, it was only about 230 pounds, which is fully a fourth less. On the other hand, the average American is now eating nearly a third more sugar, probably a fourth more milk and dairy products, nearly a fifth more meat, possibly a fifth more vegetables, and a tenth more fruit.

The decrease in the United States since the war years in

---

[1] See Kucynski, Robert R.—"The Balance of Births and Deaths, Vol. I, Northern and Western Europe." The Brookings Institution Investigations, published by the Macmillan Company.

consumption per person of cereal foods, principally wheat flour and cornmeal, has reduced the area of these crops needed to feed a person by about one-twelfth of an acre; while the increase in the consumption of milk, vegetables, fruits, and meat would have increased the area per person needed to produce these products by a quarter of an acre. Nearly all the increase in sugar consumption has come from Cuba, Porto Rico, Hawaii, and the Philippines, so it has not been included in the estimate. The net result, therefore, of the change in diet should have been an increase in crop land needed to feed each person of about one-sixth of an acre. For a population of 120,000,000 people this is equivalent to 20,000,000 acres of crops.

Despite this more expensive diet, not only in terms of money but also of land required to produce it, and an increase of population during the decade that should have required 26,000,000 acres more of crops to produce the additional food and fiber needed, on the present basis of consumption, or about 46,000,000 acres in all, there was an actual increase in crop acreage of only 6,000,000 acres. Indeed, after the War the acreage of crops declined until 1924 and is now no larger than in 1919. In 1924 about 25,000,000 acres of plow land lay idle. The productive powers of agriculture in the United States are beyond the consumptive powers of the people, and tend to remain so. Let us consider, therefore, the fourth way of meeting the situation, namely, by a policy that will increase exports.

4. The trend of agricultural exports from the United States has remained approximately constant, with reference to the acreage of land required to produce them, during the last thirty years. Could not exports be increased? The exports of wheat and cotton are as large or larger than twenty-five to thirty years ago, but the exports of animal products, except lard, have trended downward since the War, and the imports of beef and of dairy products now slightly exceed the exports. There is a tendency, moreover, for the exports to Asia to in-

crease, and for exports to Europe to remain constant or decline. This tendency seems likely to persist, because the birth rate in all the countries of northwestern Europe has declined so rapidly since the War that it is scarcely more than sufficient to maintain a stationary population a generation hence. In England, Germany, and Sweden not enough daughters are being born to replace the mothers of the present day. On the other hand, agricultural production in Northwestern Europe, as in the United States, is increasing, apparently, more rapidly than population. Russian grain also promises to come back into the world picture. A letter recently received from a well-informed person expresses the opinion that in three or four years Russia will be exporting 150,000,000 to 200,000,000 bushels of wheat, but, he adds, "there are many ifs in Russia."

In view of these trends of population and agricultural production, it appears unlikely that any great increase in demand for American agricultural products by northwestern Europe, where most of our agricultural exports have gone heretofore, can be expected, unless a notable shift in diet from cereals to meat and other more expensive foods should occur. In southern Europe the birth rate is still high and the people might well use more agricultural products, but owing to limited natural resources it will be difficult for these nations to develop the necessary purchasing power. However, if American tourists and American capital continue to flow to Europe in increasing quantities, even southern Europe may be enabled to purchase enough farm products to materially improve our agricultural situation.

Although the immediate prospect for a notable increase of agricultural exports to Europe is rather gray, if we turn and look to the Orient there can be seen in the dim distance rays of sunshine breaking through the clouds. In Asia there are twice as many people as in Europe, with high birth rates and with no tendency toward decline, except a suggestion of such in the last three or four years in Japan. For fifty years, despite the progress of industrialization, the birth rate in Japan has been increasing, until recently; and in the few Chinese families that have been studied, an improvement in economic welfare appears to result in a larger family, rather than a smaller. These tendencies are the opposite of those in Europe and North America; and both religion and family sentiment in the Orient are so strong that it will be many decades, doubtless, before birth-control methods bring the birth rates down to the level of those in North America and northwestern Europe.

If China follows in the footsteps of Japan and develops industrially, as China has already started to do, there is a prospect not only of a notable increase in population, but also of an even greater increase in purchasing power. Japan's population has doubled in the past sixty years, and that nation has only one-fourth acre of crop land per capita as compared with one-half acre in China. The coal resources of China are vastly greater than those of Japan, and in addition to small deposits of iron there are abundant supplies available in India and elsewhere. The innate intelligence and industry of the Chinese people is probably equal to that of any large group of people in the world. The problem in the Orient, even more than in Europe, is that of developing the purchasing power of the people, which means producing power and exporting power. The industrial development of China appears to the writer the brightest spot on the horizon of American agriculture. The vast shipments of silk, pottery and toys from Japan to the United States have been not a small factor in that Island Empire's industrial development, and have enabled her to buy cotton and rice and many other things from our farmers. Japanese mills now consume as much cotton as those of England, and this is only an inkling of what may happen in the Orient when China becomes stabilized politically, adopts the panoply of science, and develops into an industrial nation. But it must be realized that the industrial development of a nation is a slow process, and that the export of farm products to the Orient are not likely to exceed those to Europe much before the time when the population of the United States becomes stationary.

Those who are interested in the future welfare of American agriculture may find comfort in this fact, that the areas of cultivable land in North America, in Europe including the U.S.S.R., and in eastern and southern Asia are comparable in magnitude, probably 1,500,000,000 acres, more or less, in each of the three areas. But the population of these three areas is as 1 to 3½ to 7, and this ratio seems likely to increase rather than diminish. On the one side of the Pacific are a billion people, on the other side about 150,000,000 (excluding South America); and the two groups of peoples cultivate much the same area of land and produce much the same quantity of agricultural products. On the one side of the Pacific millions of people, mostly farmers and their families, are often hungry and sometimes perish of starvation, while on the other side of the ocean less than one-tenth as many farmers are producing more food and fibers than the people of the Continent can consume, and are suffering from a surplus. Clearly America and Asia are complementary in their conditions, and certainly the exchange of American food for Asiatic silks and art products, pottery, toys and other manufactured goods, should increase with the passage of time. The interrelationships of the Pacific peoples is one of the great economic problems of the world, and in its solution American farmers ultimately may find the solution for their problems also.

A NEW NATIONAL LAND POLICY

Meanwhile relief for American agriculture, it appears, must be found largely at home. One of the ways to improve the situation is through a new national land policy. Although the upward trend in number of beef cattle, and the probability of a similar upward trend in number of hogs, suggests the likelihood of a gradual and slight increase in acreage of crop land during the next few years, most of this increase doubtless will occur, as it has been occurring since the War, in the Great Plains region and the Northwest, and most of the 20 to 25 million acres of plow land lying idle in the southern and eastern States will continue to lie idle.

A classification of the land in these States especially is needed as a basis for a national land policy, which should be developed in cooperation with the States. Some of this poorer quality of farm land should doubtless be converted into forest, some might be used for pasture, and probably some should be retained in crops. "The basis of such a classification" as the Secretary of Agriculture says in his last (1929) report, "would be definite information concerning the physical characteristics of various types of land. Physical and economic information thus assembled and organized would make it possible to determine whether areas of impoverished or decadent agriculture could be restored to prosperity by a reorganization of farming. For farming areas which could not be thus restored, the determination of the fact would indicate the true course to follow. It would also facilitate a program of regrouping population in sparsely settled areas so as to economize expenditures for schools, roads, and other utilities. The economic possibilities of areas hitherto not employed for agriculture might also be determined.

"What can be done and should be done immediately is to recognize that there is a great problem of land use, that an early attack upon it is essential, that research is needed in diversified fields, and that it should be carried on systematically under a unified plan of coordinated action."

VIII

LAND WASTAGE ENCOURAGES OVERPRODUCTION

By Dr. J. G. LIPMAN

Director, New Jersey Agricultural Experiment Station

LAND has been used in this country for tilled crops where it should have been reserved for forests and range. Much of our potentially arable land was brought into production too soon and, to that extent we have wasted it. Cut-over and range land of marginal quality, at best, was turned by the plow and entered into unfair competition with land legitimately usable for crop production.

The lavish expenditure of land and soil capital has marked the economic progress of the nation. We have overgrazed the range; we have wasted plant-food by excessive soil leaching; we have made alkali flats out of some of our finest irrigated land. The organic matter which a long succession of centuries had stored in our surface soils has been destroyed, in large measure, by forest and prairie fires and by the intensified activities of soil bacteria and fungi. Silt and clay and dissolved salts are constantly moving to lower altitudes and to the sea. This moving we have speeded up.

EXTENT OF SOIL WASTAGE

The cultivated crops in the United States removed in 1927 approximately 32.5 pounds of nitrogen, 12.5 pounds of phosphoric acid, 30.75 pounds of potash, and 13 pounds of lime per acre. The nitrogen loss approximates 9,000,000 tons per annum. This loss is offset, in part, by the nitrogen returned to the land in farmyard manure, by the fixation of nitrogen by bacteria associated with clover and other legumes, and by bacteria in the soil-fixing nitrogen independently of association with legumes. After due credit is allowed for the nitrogen returned to the land in animal manures, for that fixed by bacteria and that brought down by rain and other atmospheric precipitation, there is still a net loss of 3,000,000 to 4,000,000 tons of nitrogen annually in 300,000,000 acres of arable land. It is evident, therefore, that we suffer terrific wastage of nitrogen, and that our methods of soil management, especially from the point of view of using more lime and of fixing more nitrogen with the aid of bacteria, should be rationalized and made more effective. This is particularly important since we apply in commercial fertilizers less than 300,000 tons of nitrogen annually. Estimates for 1928–1929 show a world production somewhat more than 2,000,000 tons of chemical nitrogen. Of this amount, 1,684,000 tons were presumably available for agricultural uses. As the chemical fixation of atmospheric nitrogen expands and our crop production methods are intensified, there will be more nitrogen applied to the soil in the form of chemical fertilizers. None the less, we shall always depend in large measure on conservation methods as well as on biological fixation for maintaining economically an adequate supply of nitrogen in our soils and for producing animal and human food at a reasonable cost.

Aside from the losses of plant-food caused by the harvesting of crops, there are very extensive losses brought about by erosion. It is estimated by Bennett that erosion removes annually 1,500,000,000 tons of soil material. On the basis of the analyses of 389 samples of surface soil, he estimates that the material removed by erosion contains the following percentages of plant-food:

	%
Nitrogen	0.10
Phosphoric Acid	0.15
Potash	1.55
Lime	1.56
Magnesia	0.84
Total	4.20

(not including sulphur)

It would seem, therefore, that the 1,500,000,000 tons of soil material removed in suspension by running water contains 63,000,000 tons of plant-food.

In summarizing the experiments carried on at the Missouri Experiment Station over a period of years, Miller shows that there has been an annual loss of about 40 tons of soil material per acre where the land was plowed but kept free of vegetation. Where the land was continuously in corn, the average loss chargeable to erosion was equivalent to about 17 tons per acre. On the other hand, where the land was kept in grass continuously, the annual loss was equivalent to only one-quarter of a ton per annum. Miller estimates, therefore, that, under the conditions of his experiments, the land with a slope of 3.68 per cent would lose 7 inches of surface soil in 26 years where the land is tilled but not cropped. Under the same conditions, land kept continually under grass would lose 7 inches of surface material in four thousand years. According to estimates of the time involved in the formation of soil, surface wastage should not exceed some such rate as one inch in a thousand years.

HOW THE WASTAGE MAY BE AVOIDED

The Bad Lands of China or the bare hillsides of Palestine are a good example of the irreparable damage done by erosion and chemical denudation. The removal of the surface material not only destroys more or less extensive areas, but leads to the silting in of streams, the changing of the course of rivers, the formation of swamps, the spread of malaria, and beyond that, extensive flood damage. Thus the forests on the steeper slopes are the most effective check on soil erosion. On the less steep slopes, the grass cover is as effective. Hence in any sound national policy of land utilization, provision should be made for the protection of the land by means of forests and grass-lands wherever these may seem necessary. Beyond that, the construction of terrace, the suitable rotation of crops, the use of lime for making the soil more mellow and more pervious, the lessening of the run-off and the storing of a greater amount of water in the soil itself should be properly considered in developing an effective land utilization policy.

Average land of good quality contains approximately one ton each of nitrogen and phosphoric acid per acre in the surface 7 inches. The same land should contain 10 to 20 tons of potash, 5 to 10 tons of lime and 4 to 5 tons of magnesia. There should also be in it approximately one-quarter of a ton each of magnesia and sulphur. In heavier and richer soils, the amounts of these constituents may be substantially larger. In the lighter, sandy soils there would be considerably less. But, altogether, we have in our soils a vast deposit of plant-food which should be used economically and effectively and should be conserved for the days to come.

Since our soils are one of the greatest of our natural resources and since the present and future welfare of the nation must depend on the effective use of our soil resources, too much thought cannot be given to a most thorough-going study of land utilization policies, the protection of our soils against erosion and chemical denudation, the elimination of marginal areas as a competitive factor in building a prosperous agriculture, and the devising of systems of soil and farm management that will help toward the production of adequate supplies of human and animal food for our growing population. The supply of such food should be satisfactory not alone from the standpoint of quantity, but should also be of such quality as to permit of the best dietary standards for the development of individuals possessing the maximum of vigor and disease resistance.

When we relieve the good agricultural land from the unfair and destructive competition of marginal acres, we shall point the way to a more prosperous agriculture.

IX

OVERPRODUCTION IN THE RADIO INDUSTRY

By HERBERT H. FROST

President Utah Radio Products Co.; Chairman Merchandising Committee, Radio Mfrs. Association; President R.M.A. 1924–1928–1929

BROADCASTING, as it is known today, was first offered to the public in 1921, and was the result of many years of research and development on the part of radio and electrical engineers in the United States and abroad. From 1921 until 1930 the number of broadcasting stations increased from one to six hundred, located from coast to coast and bringing programs to every city, town, and hamlet within our borders.

The appeal of this new adaptation of science to the American home immediately gripped the imagination of the masses and resulted in a demand for radio receiving sets, tubes, parts, and accessories.

This demand started at a time of general business depression and, therefore, attracted all types of manufacturers seeking something to put into factories facing lay-offs and shutdowns.

Wholesalers and retailers in many lines were also seeking merchandise to boost declining sales curves, and radio was seized upon as a great opportunity. Manufacturers of automobile accessories, electrical merchandise, hardware, clothing, gasoline engines, etc., became radio manufacturers almost over night. Wholesalers and retailers in the same fields, as well as jewelers, barber shops, etc., became engaged in radio distribution. In addition, many new manufacturing companies were formed to make radio only, and exclusive radio wholesalers began to appear all over the country. This condition, naturally, brought the manufacturers, jobbers, and dealers together in a united effort to supply the ever-increasing consumer demand. Little, or no attention, was given to trade practices, sales policies, or good management. Every effort was bent in the direction of securing raw material and turning it into finished products.

Distribution was thus started through wholesale channels and in turn from the wholesaler to the retailer. Retailers of all kinds became radio stores over night. Trade names were only in the making, and the public bought everything in sight, regardless of price, appearance, or performance.

Such a situation cannot prevail over any long period and about June, 1925, the trade and the public were beginning to recognize trade names behind the products and to demand good merchandise, properly merchandised.

The year 1926 brought new names to the fore and the radio dealer, as well as the public, began to think of the stability and reputation of the manufacturer in determining purchases. At this period, the manufacturing division of the industry expanded tremendously. Millions of dollars were put in for additional working capital to increase production and sales of complete radio sets, parts, tubes, and accessories.

During this entire period, the technical branch of the industry had not been asleep. As improvements were made and embodied in receiving sets, the public was told of "new and revolutionary developments." This led to a race between manufacturers to "beat the gun" and constantly produce something new. Obviously, a race of this kind brings on obsolescence, resulting in inventory losses, liquidations, and uncertainty.

About the middle of the year 1928, great improvements in merchandising methods began to be felt and there seemed to be a general feeling that the radio industry had begun to stabilize. Manufacturers were producing better values, wholesalers and retailers were equipped to handle time payments, make proper installations, etc.

Then came the era of "easy money" and the radio manufacturer found the public eager to invest in the radio industry. This great boom of general buying and prosperity raised the tempo of the radio manufacturer to the highest pitch. Sales schedules and manufacturing schedules were planned and executed far beyond what later proved to be any reasonable point of expectancy.

By September, 1929, it was evident that the tide was turning and many manufacturers began to revise their plans accordingly. In many cases, however, the action was taken too late, and by November 1st the manufacturing branch of the radio industry showed glaring signs of weakness in many places. Manufacturers with adequate finance managed to weather the storm, while those not so fortunate went into the hands of creditors, committees, or receiverships. Wholesalers and retailers became demoralized and looked in vain for something from the manufacturers to save the situation. Frozen credits rapidly mounted into millions of dollars.

The general plan of distribution in effect did not help the situation that prevailed in the manufacturing branch. Wholesalers found it necessary to discontinue purchases, leaving the manufacturers in many cases without distribution at a time when it was greatly needed. Retail outlets always "played the field," that is to say, the retailers have never been an agent for any particular brand of radios, but by and large, have followed the trend of public opinion and handled the brands in "spot demand." Needless to say, this situation presented the most serious problem to the manufacturer. Dealer distribution of the type and under policies used in the automotive field, wherein the dealer agent has an obligation under the sales agreement, would have a most desirable effect on the radio industry.

At this writing, the situation in the radio industry is much improved.

1. Distressed merchandise in the form of inventories of old sets, etc., has been sold.

2. Through consolidation, many concerns have been strengthened and find themselves in an enviable market position.

3. Many weaker units have eliminated themselves.

4. Manufacturers are proceeding on a sounder basis as regards production and sales.

5. The experience of last year has been indelibly impressed on the industry.

The public recognizes radio today as a necessity (education-advertising). Bankers, finance companies, and business men find the radio industry facing the future with a determination to build and sell at a fair profit and in quantities dictated by careful market analysis and good judgment.

Radio has arrived and taken its place with the other great American industries. We face, however, with these industries the task of bringing potential output into closer relation with normal demand. The accumulation on a national scale of a margin of excess capacity, is far different from the accumulation of temporary surpluses. Temporary surpluses lend themselves to absorption. Idle capacity is a continual drag. It encourages wasteful producers and distributors to enter the field, regardless of the ability of existing manufacturers, wholesalers, and retailers to care for the demand. Before encouraging further expansion, let us secure an approximate idea of the potential capacity of the radio industry.

X

BALANCED PROSPERITY

By CHARLES F. ABBOTT

Executive Director, American Institute of Steel Construction

LABOR, industry, and capital are all equally concerned in the present emergency. If we are to have a happy country we must permit economic conditions which promise prosperity to business. Men are prohibited from stealing one from another, but there is no mandate against glutting the market of a competitor. Men are prohibited from committing a murder, yet no statute forbids a business engaging in practices calculated to kill off a competitor.

It is certainly the part of wisdom in this country to have our resources of oil, copper, or other basic commodities judiciously used, rather than to make them very cheap at one moment with widespread waste, and their application to uses for which some other material would be preferable.

The world's potential supply of iron ore is not inexhaustible. If the remaining ore deposits are to be conserved, if their economic development is to be assured, iron and steel products should command prices more in keeping with their intrinsic values. Otherwise our immediate profits are unreal, as they make no provision for the cost of conservation; no provision for the future.

We cannot expect industrial prosperity unless all industry is prosperous. Society, with labor included, is advanced when industry prospers and both suffer when operations continue without a reasonable profit. Destructive methods that are prevalent in many industries dissipate the profits, as price-cutting and selfishness place business at any price ahead of all other motives.

The steel constructor is just as much a victim to these general economic conditions as the man engaged in any line of business endeavor. In all industries there are a few characteristics which seemingly set them apart from other lines of business. Mass production has been introduced successfully in only a few lines. There is still a great volume of business done only on a contract basis, and handicraft has not completely passed out of the picture. But when we analyze these differences we come back once more to the original conclusion that fundamentally the same disturbing factors which are causing trouble in basic lines are equally disturbing to all businesses.

It is pretty generally obvious to those engaged in steel construction that the industry does not always follow the normal trend of business. There is usually a lag of several months, because this is a contract business which does not immediately respond to panics and fears, nor immediately to booms and emotions. The bridge builder or the fabricator as he was once called (the proper term is steel constructor) is engaged in engineering and contracting. His shop does not produce en masse. The steel constructor does not manufacture for stock and his supplies do not have the habit of accumulating during periods of depression.

The steel constructor purchases supplies of structural steel from the mills mostly against orders he actually has in hand for the framing of buildings and bridges. His sales to owners are based upon the current price of the raw material—structural steel—and the cost of fabricating it into the shapes for the particular job. All the sales are against specification and on contract. For that reason the reported volume of business done by this industry will not immediately reflect the condition of business generally.

While it might seem, therefore, that the structural steel industry is peculiarly free of the normal gluts and famines of business, that is true only in theory. The shops of the steel constructors are usually designed to care for a certain amount of business monthly. Machinery and staff are capable of handling a designated tonnage. In some instances this means that the shop is prepared to bid only on the smaller construction jobs because they involve the smaller tonnage, and the small shops afford a flexible organization just suited to that purpose. On the other hand another shop is equipped with machinery and men capable of handling a much larger tonnage monthly. Such a shop under ordinary circumstances would bid only on the heavy or the large construction jobs requiring a large organization to carry out the contract in good time.

When business becomes extremely bad and there is no recovery in sight, normal safeguards are thrown to the winds. Then competition between the shops of differing sizes becomes actual and a chaotic condition results. In order to safeguard the industry it is always wise to do everything possible to prevent any such thing happening. Today we are seemingly far removed from such an eventuality. In 1921 a total of 1,188,600 tons of steel construction was sold in the United States. During 1929, the business amounted to 3,842,300 tons. This great increase represents a constant and a gradual growth. It was brought about by no usual method, but rather represents the result of a jointed and cooperative effort of the industry as a whole.

The American Institute of Steel Construction was created by the steel constructors back in 1921 as an agency for standardizing structual shapes and for defining standards of steel construction. Once that objective was achieved it was determined that the Institute should bend its efforts towards developing the market for steel construction in bridges and buildings. It has done much more than that, it has developed new markets for the material and the services of the industry. Steel frame houses, traffic viaducts, hydraulic irrigation dams, hangars, piling, steel floors, and other new developments came in for promotion and each have contributed additional tonnage work to the steel constructor.

OVERPRODUCTION

Mass production is predicated upon constant production, and it is expensive if the operation is halted or stopped. Under such a system it not infrequently happens that 50 per cent of the cost of an article is due to plant stoppage, for that cost continues no matter whether the plant is in operation or not. That is why a plant is often encouraged to sell its output at a loss. It is that much more reason why we should take steps to cut those losses before they start, to appraise most carefully the absorptive capacity of the market for the article produced. If the planning is done correctly we can avoid the loss and insure the plant of continuous operation when keyed to meet the demand and not to exceed it.

It is easy to cut a price, but it is difficult to reconstruct the price structure after it has once been pulled down. The constant lowering of prices is an endless process. In this downward trend of prices there comes a time when the selling prices are below the cost of production, profits are dissipated, and the business is being transacted at a loss. In this wild scramble for volume, industry must learn that distress lurks just ahead and the only remedy lies in the rationalization of output.

Overproduction not only invites bankruptcy for the industry overproducing, but also encourages bankruptcy among those who consume the output of that industry. And bankruptcy is one of the greatest industrial wastes that we have to contend with today.

Modern statesmanship must take this fact into consideration. In preaching the merits of rationalized output, we are but preaching a better industrial life, we are merely encouraging some kind of a uniformity of success and pointing the way to the removal of waste.

We have the merits of cost accounting hurled at us from time to time. There is a good deal of truth in the claim that producers should know their costs if they would do business on a successful basis. That is axiomatic, but it goes only half the way; knowing our costs is but the first step. The second is to know our market. But even assuming that we know both, it is of little avail unless we act upon the information that has been given us. We must rationalize the output. We must equal production with consumption, and thereby do away with periodic slumps, unemployment, and reduced buying power.

STABILIZED PRODUCTION

Stabilized production would do more to improve prices and profits, to eliminate destructive forms of competition than any other influence that can be brought to bear. It is the key to the greater prosperity and the market is the direct approach through which research, advertising, and educational promotional effort would complete the answer.

Congress has authorized a census of distribution. Unconsciously that gives official sanction to a new science, the science of rationing output to consumption. We have awakened to the necessity of putting a curb on selfishness and of ridding industry generally of the tremendous wastes in marketing produce. The day is rapidly approaching when we have every reason to expect to have a rationalization of output to consumption. We are only beginning to discover means of measuring the volume of the market potentiality. We have yet to develop that method of regulating production to consumption capacity. When we reach that point we will have devised a scientific rationalizing of output.

We are forbidden to advise competitors on selling prices, but on the other hand we might feasibly advise each other as to expansion of productive capacity.

Excess and idle capacity represents a loss of time and energy involved in its creation. The public which buys the output of the active portion of an industry is compelled to pay the carrying charges for the idle portion. The system is economically unsound.

XI

AMERICA'S PLACE IN WORLD COMMERCE A CENTURY AGO AND NOW

By HENRY CHALMERS

Chief, Division of Foreign Tariffs, United States Department of Commerce

SMALL in volume, simple in nature, and limited in range as the American foreign trade of 100 years ago must seem compared with that of modern days, it should be remembered that world commerce generally was not highly developed in 1830. The means of transportation then available and the costliness of it limited the range of profitable commerce largely to "colonial goods," to textiles, and a few other types of manufactured wares. The bulk movement of staple foodstuffs, minerals, and heavy manufactures was not to come until the application of steam had considerably cheapened transportation costs, both on land and on sea. The international specialization or division of labor that makes the world economic organization of today, and produces the tremendous volumes that move in international trade, was not then possible. Each country had to content itself largely with what could possibly be produced within its own borders.

The aggregate value of the total international trade in 1830 was less than two billion dollars ($1,980 millions). In relation to this comparatively limited volume of world commerce, the foreign trade developed by the vigorous young American republic already entitled her in those days to sixth place among the commercial nations, according to the best records of early trade available. England was the undisputed leader as a world trader, with a combined total of imports and exports during 1830 of $428 millions or nearly 23 per cent of the world total. The German traders of the Hanse Towns were a distant second, their turnover amounting to 224 millions.

French ports on the Atlantic and Mediterranean together took third place, with a commerce of $200 millions. The traders of Holland and Belgium (then united), were fourth in volume of their foreign operations, with $146 millions; Russia ranked fifth with $136 millions, and the United States followed close with a total foreign trade during 1830 of $134 millions. No other country, according to the earlier records, showed a total annual trade at that time of as much as 100 millions. The rather important commercial place that the young nation had already won was also indicated from the fact that, largely as a result of the stimulation to her shipbuilding during the Napoleonic Wars, fully 87 per cent of her exports and 93 per cent of her imports during 1830 were carried in American vessels.

World commerce—in the volume, variety, and breadth which we know today—may be said to be practically the creation of the past century. In 1830 the combined foreign commerce of the countries of the world, which had been growing but slowly during the generations preceding, totaled—as already indicated—less than 2 billion dollars in value. During 1928, the last year for which a reliable estimate is available, the total value of world commerce was estimated at $68 billions, an increase of about thirty-five fold. When it is remembered that the foreign commerce of the United States during the period increased about twice as fast as did the commerce of the world as a whole, some indication is afforded of the exceptional rate of progress of the United States during a century of tremendous advance on the part of the world generally.

Viewing American commerce during 1929, the last year of this century, we find the United States rivaling Great Britain

THE CENTURY'S CHANGES IN THE

A brief retrospect of the economic and commercial progress of the United States during the past hundred years may be afforded by selecting a number of significant measures of such progress and viewing their ad-

TABLE

SIGNIFICANT MEASURES OF ECONOMIC PROGRESS OF

(Calendar years are shown unless otherwise indicated. With few exceptions figures federal sources)

Year	Continental Area (Thousands of Sq. Mi.)	Population (Millions)	Railway Mileage (Miles Owned)	Railway Freight: Tons Carried One Mile (Millions)	Electric Current Produced by Central Stations (Millions of Kw-hrs.)	Production		
						Cotton (Thousands of 500-pound Bales)	Wheat (Millions of Bushels)	Coal (Millions of Short Tons)
		(1)	(2)	(3)	(4)	(5)		
1830	1,792	13	23	....	....	732	65	0.3
1840	1,792	17	2,818	....	....	1,348	85	2
1850	2,997	23	9,021	....	....	2,136	100	7
1860	3,027	32	30,626	....	....	3,841	173	15
1870	3,027	39	52,922	....	....	4,025	236	33
1880	3,027	50	93,267	32,349	....	6,357	499	71
1890	3,027	63	163,597	77,207	....	8,562	378	158
1900	3,027	76	193,346	141,597	4,768	10,123	603	270
1910	3,027	92	240,293	255,017	17,572	11,609	635	502
1920	3,027	106	252,845	413,699	43,555	13,440	833	658
1929	3,027	122	249,309	450,390	97,296	14,919	807	609

(1) Estimates as of July 1.

(2) The last figure in this column is for 1928, not 1929.

(3) 1880 to 1910 are fiscal years ended June 30; 1929 is estimate based on figures for Class I Railways.

(4) Figures in this column for 1900 and 1910 are actually figures for 1902 and 1912, respectively.

(5) The figure 65 for 1830 is an unofficial estimate; those for 1840, 1850, 1860 are census figures for the crop of the previous year in each case.

(6) The figure for 1929 is from American Iron and Steel Institute.

CHARACTER OF AMERICAN FOREIGN TRADE

vance from decade to decade. This has been attempted in the following composite table:

I

THE UNITED STATES DURING THE PAST CENTURY: 1830–1929

are drawn from the Statistical Abstract of the United States, and other official

Production		Manufactures: Values Added to Materials by Manufacture (Millions of Dollars)	General Imports (Millions of Dollars)	Domestic Exports (Millions of Dollars)	Re-exports (Millions of Dollars)	Merchant Marine	
Pig Iron (Millions of Long Tons)	Crude Petroleum (Millions of Barrels)					Sailing Vessels (Thousands of Gross Tons)	Steam and Motor Vessels (Thousands of Gross Tons)
(6)		(7)	(8)	(8)	(8)	(9)	(9)
0.2	....	....	63	59	13	1,127	64
0.3	....	....	98	112	12	1,978	202
0.6	....	464	173	135	9	3,010	526
0.8	0.5	854	354	316	17	4,486	868
2	5	1,395	461	388	16	3,171	1,075
4	26	1,973	697	876	14	2,856	1,212
9	46	4,210	823	846	12	2,565	1,859
14	64	4,831	829	1,453	25	2,507	2,658
27	210	8,529	1,563	1,829	37	2,608	4,900
37	443	24,803	5,278	8,080	148	2,501	13,823
42	1,006	27,585	4,400	5,157	84	2,315	14,162

(7) Census figures covering operations of previous year in each case, except the last figure which is for 1927.

(8) Figures for 1830 and 1840 are for fiscal years ended September 30; figures for 1850 and 1860 are for fiscal years ended June 30. The statistics of the foreign commerce of the United States include the trade of the customs districts of Alaska, Hawaii, and Porto Rico with foreign countries, but not the trade of these territories with the United States. The exclusion of imports of Alaska, Hawaii, and Porto Rico from foreign countries, or shipments to those countries, would reduce the figures shown in the above table only slightly.

(9) Figures are for fiscal years except 1830 and 1840.

for the position of the greatest foreign trading nation. The year's exports of domestic products from the United States valued at $5,157 millions, and the imports at $4,400 millions, with a relatively small re-export trade of $84 millions. If the handling of foreign goods for re-export be excluded from consideration, the United States is now seen to rank first among the nations, and above Great Britain, in the combined value of annual domestic exports and imports for consumption. Germany now ranks third among world traders, although at a distance behind the two leaders; France holds fourth place, with Canada and British India ranking fifth and sixth.

In contrast with a century ago, when only six countries had a foreign trade valued annually at as much as 100 million dollars, there are now fourteen countries, each of whose total annual foreign commerce has been valued at over one billion dollars during recent years. In addition to the countries named above, they are ranked in the order of value during 1928, Japan, Italy, Netherlands, Argentina, Belgium, Australia, Czechoslovakia, and Netherland East Indies.

An examination of the nature of the commodities making up our current export and import trade, as compared with a century ago, is highly significant. Not only does it bring out the great unfolding of the country during that period, and the transition that has been taking place from an agricultural to an industrial nation, but it indicates the probable trend for some time ahead.

The most significant feature of our export trade has been the shift from the dominance of raw materials or natural products, as our principal contribution to world markets, to manufactured or processed goods. Whereas in 1830 crude materials made up the largest part of our exports (63 per cent), the surplus of such materials sent abroad in recent years —while now very much larger in amount than then—makes up less than one-quarter (22 per cent in 1929) of our present export trade, broadened and enlarged as that has been by the rapidly increasing volume of manufactured goods of every category. Where in 1830 finished manufactures constituted but 10 per cent of the small total of exports of those days, practically half (49 per cent) of our total exports during 1929 were made up of such finished manufactures. If to this class is added the semi-manufactures, as also products of industry, manufacturing is seen to have contributed two-thirds of the total export trade of the country last year.

Foodstuffs, either in the crude or processed condition, have been a somewhat fluctuating element in our exports. For a time they rose into high prominence. During the decades following the Civil War, the ready outlets to markets created by the expanding network of railways over the Middle West, joined with the cheapening of ocean transportation by steamships, stimulated the rapid taking up of the fertile farm lands of the Mississippi Valley for the growing of grain and the raising of livestock, largely for sale in the markets of the Old World. For a short time, the combined exports of breadstuffs and provisions overtopped even cotton in value. For the last two or three decades, however, they have been declining in importance among our exports (the World War period excepted), as the needs of the increasing domestic population are leaving a smaller food surplus to be disposed of abroad.

The position of the United States in the international division of labor, as primarily a purveyor of raw materials and foodstuffs to the foreign countries—who could thereby devote their energies more largely to manufacturing in its various branches—has been undergoing an important change over a period of several decades. The absolute quantity of cotton, or grain, or petroleum exported from the United States may not have declined in amount, but so distinctly has the United States found its comparative advantages in the more advanced economic activities, that our growing population and new

LEADING COMMODITIES IN EXPORT TRADE OF THE UNITED STATES
1929 COMPARED WITH 1830
(Arranged in Order of Value in Each Period)

1929

COMMODITY	VALUE
Cotton, unmanufactured	$770,800,000
Machinery*	612,700,000
Industrial	*277,800,000*
Agricultural, and implements	*140,800,000*
Electrical, and apparatus	*121,400,000*
Petroleum and products	561,200,000
Refined oils	*493,400,000*
Crude oils	*37,800,000*
Automobiles, parts and accessories	539,300,000
Passenger cars, and trucks	*345,700,000*
Packing-house products	202,800,000
Meat-products	*78,800,000*
Fats and oils	*124,100,000*
Lard	*105,500,000*
Iron and steel-mill products	200,100,000
Wheat, including flour	192,300,000
Wheat, grain	*111,500,000*
Copper, including ore and manufactures	183,400,000
Chemical and related products	152,100,000
Chemicals (coal tar, industrial, medicinal)	*82,000,000*
Pigments, paints, varnishes	*29,100,000*
Tobacco, unmanufactured	146,100,000
Fruits and nuts	137,500,000
Cotton manufactures, including yarns	135,100,000
Cloth, duck, tire fabrics	*79,400,000*
Sawmill products	110,600,000
Boards and timber	*109,800,000*
Coal and coke	106,200,000
Iron and steel advanced manufactures	87,000,000
Rubber and manufactures	77,000,000
Automobile casings	*33,500,000*
Leather	42,900,000
Wood manufactures, advanced	40,900,000
Paper and manufactures	37,200,000
Furs and manufactures	35,700,000
Corn (grain)	34,100,000
Photographic and projection goods	31,600,000
Naval stores, gums, and resins	31,000,000
Oil cake and meal	28,400,000
Barley and malt	27,500,000
Books and printed matter	27,100,000
Vegetables and preparations	25,300,000
Fish	23,500,000
Silk manufactures	20,400,000
Tobacco manufactures	19,500,000
Musical instruments	18,900,000
Dairy products	17,900,000
Leather manufactures	17,700,000
Sulphur or brimstone, crude, in lumps	17,600,000
Brass and bronze	17,500,000

1929 (*continued*)

COMMODITY	VALUE
Railway cars and parts	$16,900,000
Logs and other unmanufactured wood	15,300,000
Rice and rice flour, etc	14,100,000
Clay and clay products	12,700,000
Scientific and professional instruments, apparatus and supplies	12,400,000

Total 40 specified items (93.1 per cent) $4,800,300,000

GRAND TOTAL ALL EXPORTS (U. S. Merchandise) $5,157,100,000

1830

COMMODITY	VALUE
Cotton	$29,675,000
Wheat and flour	6,132,000
Wheat	*46,000*
Tobacco	5,586,000
Animal products	2,175,000
Beef, tallow, hides, and horned cattle	*718,000*
Pork (pickled), bacon, lard, live hogs	*1,315,000*
Butter and cheese	*142,000*
Rice	1,987,000
Lumber (staves, shingles, boards, etc.)	1,650,000
Chemical products	1,485,000
Medicinal drugs	*92,000*
Ginseng	*68,000*
Oak bark and other dye	*220,000*
Ashes	*1,105,000*
Cotton manufactures	1,318,000
Fish (dried and pickled)	757,000
Skins and furs	642,000
Soap and tallow candles	619,000
Indian corn and meal	597,000
Whale and other fish oil	568,000
Manufactures of wood	412,000
Leather boots and shoes	339,000
Naval stores, tar, pitch, resin, and turpentine	321,000
Iron and steel manufactures	309,000
Hats	309,000
Spermaceti candles	249,000
Snuff and other tobacco manufactures	247,000

Total 20 specified items (94.6 per cent) $55,377,000

GRAND TOTAL ALL EXPORTS (U. S. Merchandise) $58,525,000

* Includes office and printing machinery.

LEADING COMMODITIES IN IMPORT TRADE OF THE UNITED STATES
1929 COMPARED WITH 1830
(Arranged in Order of Value in Each Period)

1929

COMMODITY	VALUE
Silk, raw	$427,100,000
Coffee	302,400,000
Rubber, crude	241,000,000
Sugar, cane	209,300,000
Paper and manufactures	163,400,000
Newsprint	*144,500,000*
Copper, including ore and manufactures	153,700,000
Chemicals and related products	144,100,000
Chemicals (coal tar, industrial, medicinal)	*59,900,000*
Fertilizers	*72,300,000*
Petroleum and products	143,500,000
Crude oil	*79,900,000*
Refined oils	*61,000,000*
Hides and skins	137,300,000
Furs and manufactures	122,500,000
Paper base stocks	118,100,000
Wood pulp	*88,600,000*
Vegetable oils, expressed, and fats	100,700,000
Tin (bars, blocks, pigs)	91,800,000
Wool and mohair	87,300,000
Fruits and nuts	86,900,000
Art works	82,100,000
Oilseeds	79,300,000
Flaxseed	*46,500,000*
Wool manufactures, including yarns, etc	78,500,000
Burlaps	77,400,000
Cotton manufactures, including yarns, etc	69,300,000
Diamonds	56,000,000
Sawmill products	54,200,000
Boards, planks, deals	*43,300,000*
Tobacco, unmanufactured	53,800,000
Cotton, unmanufactured	53,300,000
Cocoa or cacao beans	49,500,000
Vegetables and preparations	47,800,000
Flax, hemp, and ramie manufactures	47,400,000
Iron ore and manufactures of iron and steel	46,300,000
Leather	44,600,000
Machinery and vehicles	42,200,000
Leather manufactures	41,600,000
Meat products	40,900,000
Manila, istle, sisal, and other unmanufactured vegetable fibers	40,200,000

1929 (*Continued*)

COMMODITY	VALUE
Fish	$39,800,000
Silk manufactures	39,000,000
Varnish gums and other resins and balsams, n.e.s.	35,600,000
Dairy products	30,400,000
Tea	25,900,000
Clay and clay products	24,400,000
Ferro alloys	23,500,000
Total 40 specified items (85.3 cent)	**$3,752,100,000**
GRAND TOTAL ALL IMPORTS	**$4,399,400,000**

1830

COMMODITY	VALUE
Cotton manufactures	$7,865,000
Iron and steel manufactures	6,144,000
Wool manufactures	5,901,000
Silks from India and other silk manufactures	5,813,000
Sugar	4,631,000
Coffee	4,227,000
Flax, hemp, and ramie manufactures	3,958,000
Tea	2,425,000
Hides and skins	2,410,000
Wines, liquors, and spirits	2,254,000
Pottery	1,451,000
Molasses	996,000
Laces (of thread, silk or cotton, and coach)	828,000
Copper and manufactures	807,000
Indigo	716,000
Salt	672,000
Fruits	520,000
Leather, and manufactures	500,000
Spices	458,000
Glass and glassware	391,000
Total 20 specified items (84.4 per cent)	**$52,967,000**
GRAND TOTAL ALL IMPORTS	**$62,721,000**

efforts are being increasingly devoted to enlarging our manufacturing operations. We are right now witnessing the shift in the balance from natural products to manufactures as the class of goods that is to dominate our export trade.

On the other hand, in our import trade, there has been an almost consistent decline from decade to decade, during the past century, in the relative place of manufactured goods ready for consumption. From a situation at the beginning of the century when finished wares made up the predominant part of our imports (57 per cent), the proportion had shrunk to about 30 per cent by 1880, and during 1929 made up less than 23 per cent of the total importations.

The unparalleled expansion and diversification of manufacturing, accelerated particularly since the Civil War, has far outrun the needs of our growing population even with its rising standards. We have come not only to make ourselves most of the manufactured articles for which we were formerly dependent upon foreign countries, but in many lines we have had increasing surpluses which we could supply to the world's markets.

As a corollary to this transformation there has been a marked increase, from decade to decade, in the proportion of imports which have been made up of raw materials for manufacturing and of semi-processed commodities for the needs of our industries. From a condition a century ago when crude materials made up less than 8 per cent of our imports, and semi-processed about an equal amount, by 1929 crude materials made up 35 per cent of the much enlarged total, with semi-manufactures adding 20 per cent additional. In other words, whereas a century ago 84 per cent of our purchases from abroad were made up of foods or finished wares that went to supply the needs of consumers, a century later the majority (55 per cent) of our huge imports go to supply the needs of producers.

Expressed concretely, it is important to note that the lead-ing places among our imports are now held by our raw ma-terial requirements from abroad, namely, raw silk, crude rubber, hides and skins, crude petroleum, leaf tobacco, wool, long staple cotton, and other textile fibres, as well as by so-called "producers' materials" imported in semi-processed form, such as wood pulp, copper, burlaps, fertilizers, and chemicals. The current situation represents the attainment of the sec-ond stage in our industrial maturity. We have long passed the stage where we simply turned into finished wares for our people's consumption an increasing part of the raw materials with which our country is generously supplied. We are now reaching out increasingly to all parts of the world for sup-plies of foreign raw materials which we convert into finished goods, not alone to supply the manifold requirements and ris-ing standards of our own huge population, but to return these materials in manufactured form to the world's markets and, in most lines, to hold our own in competition with the older industrial nations.

Foodstuffs, crude and manufactured, which made up a substantial part of our imports a century ago still hold a fairly important part. They continue to be predominantly made up of very much the same types of tropical and subtropical prod-ucts, largely of semi-luxury character, which have figured in our importations all through our history—chiefly, coffee, sugar, cocoa, tea, fruits and nuts. By their nature, they are likely to continue to figure prominently among our imports.

CHANGES IN MARKETS AND SOURCES OF OUR FOREIGN TRADE

The relative present importance of various parts of the world as sources of our imports, or markets for our exports, is brought out vividly by the following diagrams from the official "Commerce Yearbook":

PERCENTAGE DISTRIBUTION OF FOREIGN TRADE IN 1929 BY CONTINENTS AND MAJOR COUNTRIES

IMPORTS

EUROPE 30.3 %
ITALY 2.7 %
FRANCE 3.9 %
GERMANY 5.8 %
UNITED KINGDOM 7.5 %
ALL OTHER 10.4 %
AFRICA 1.3 % 2.5 %
OCEANIA
ALL OTHER 6.4 %
BRITISH INDIA 3.4 %
BRI. MALAYA 5.4 %
CHINA AND HONG KONG 4.1 %
JAPAN 9.8 %
ASIA 29.1 %
CANADA 11.6 %
CUBA 4.7 %
MEXICO 2.7 %
ALL OTHER 3.4 %
NORTH AMERICA 22.3 %
ARGENTINA 2.7 %
BRAZIL 4.7 %
ALL OTHER 7.1 %
S. AMERICA 14.5 %

EXPORTS

EUROPE 45.6 %
UNITED KINGDOM 16.2 %
GERMANY 7.8 %
FRANCE 5.1 %
ITALY 2.9 %
ALL OTHER 12.7 %
AFRICA 2.5 %
OCEANIA 3.7 %
ALL OTHER 4.6 %
CHINA AND HONG KONG 2.8 %
JAPAN 4.9 %
ASIA 12.3 %
S. AMERICA 10.3 %
BRAZIL 2.1 %
ALL OTHER 4.2 %
ARGENTINA 4.0 %
ALL OTHER 3.4 %
MEXICO 2.5 %
CUBA 2.6 %
Grain via Canada 0.9 %
CANADA 17.2 %
NORTH AMERICA 25.7 %

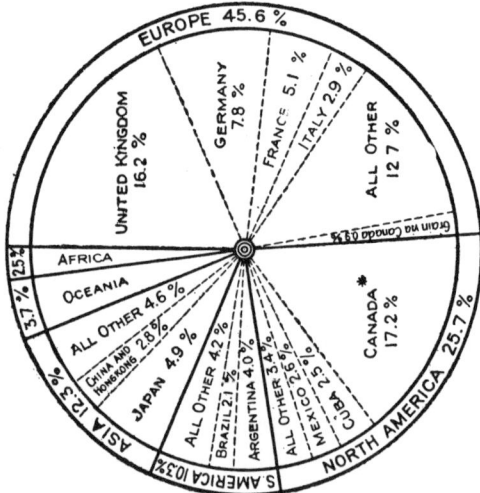

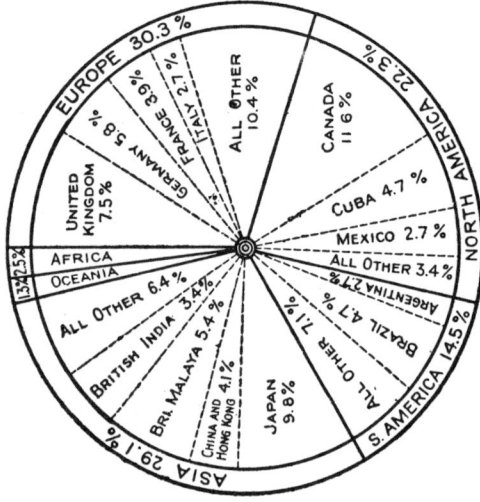

* Excluding grain exports reported as to Canada but actually in transit for Europe as shown.

* Excluding grain exports reported as to Canada but actually in transit for Europe as shown.

Europe, the market for two-thirds of our exports a century ago, and the immediate source then of almost as large a share of our imports, no longer quite so dominates our trade as it has for most of our history, although Europe still ranks first among the Continents in both aspects of our foreign trade.

As our requirements from abroad have turned increasingly to raw materials, it is natural to find our importations being drawn increasingly from the countries of Asia and of Latin America. On the other hand, as our exports have come to consist increasingly of manufactured wares, it is also natural to find our markets broadening out into countries of less-advanced industrial development. The countries of South America and of Asia, with a century ago were the markets for but one-eleventh part of our surplus production, today come nearer to taking one-quarter of our much larger exports. Perhaps even more striking has been the rise in importance of Canada from an almost negligible place among our outlets a century ago, when it was still a largely unsettled wilderness (then referred to as "Northern North America"), to a place today rivaling Great Britain as the premier foreign customer of the United States.

However, it would be a mistake to deduce that our manufactured wares do and will find markets only in the less-developed countries. A considerable part of the manufactures that the United States produces with exceptional efficiency is made up of what might be described as industrial specialties, which constitute one of our unique contributions to world commerce. These products, which frequently offer a new facility or convenience rather than displacing directly the products of other countries, often find their readiest market in the older European countries.

PLACE OF FOREIGN TRADE IN OUR NATIONAL ECONOMY

Various estimates have been presented as to the ratio of American foreign trade to the larger volume of domestic production and trade, and various have been the deductions drawn as to the consequent importance to the country of its foreign commerce. What is probably the fairest estimate places the volume of our annual exports at about 10 per cent in value of the total production of goods in the United States, with the imports only slightly less. That this ratio is not much different from what it was before the World War, despite the large increase in the absolute amounts of our exportations, reflects the increasing expansion of the general productive power of the country, with the expansion of exports keeping about the same pace.

Were the foreign markets for any one of our important export commodities to be cut off, or even temporarily checked or depressed, the repercussions upon the price of the portion sold in the domestic market, and even upon the extent of employment or general prosperity of the producers, would be of a magnitude much greater than the 10 per cent ratio might suggest.

Moreover, the 10 per cent figure represents the composite average of our whole economic output. Foreign outlets may be of minor concern to the American producers of coal, or building materials, or corn, or shoes; but they were depended upon last year as the market for the disposal of 18 per cent of our wheat, 33 per cent of our lard, 55 per cent of our cotton, 41 per cent of our leaf tobacco, about 13 per cent of our refined petroleum products, 36 per cent of our copper, 40 per cent of our typewriters, 23 per cent of our agricultural machinery, between 10 and 15 per cent of our automobiles and parts, and as much as 54 per cent of our motorcycles. The classes of commodities in which our export markets loom large presumably represent the lines in which the United States has the greatest comparative advantage in production. Even a limitation of the extent of foreign markets to the degree already attained would constitute a check to the progress of the country's development along the lines for which it apparently finds itself best suited.·

Similarly, in the matter of imports, so keen has been the competition of domestic producers for supplying the manifold needs of the American market, that the commodities making up our imports today represent a highly selected list of products, most of which this country cannot itself supply or has not found profitable to devote itself to. One needs but to visualize the paralyzing effect upon American industry and the whole continuance of our manner of living of the cutting off of ready supplies of rubber, tin, hides, silk, newsprint, or even sugar and coffee, or any of the other foreign products now the commonplace of our life, to realize the indispensable place that our import trade holds in our national economic structure and in the maintenance of the standard of civilization achieved.

SOME IMPLICATIONS IN THE TRENDS OF OUR FOREIGN TRADE

A review of the nature and trend of American international trade, as compared with a century ago, would be incomplete without some consideration of certain implications inherent in the present status of our foreign commerce and its trend towards the future. As our export trade has come to consist increasingly of manufactured goods, we have been meeting sharper competition from producers in other industrial countries—both in their home markets and in common export markets—a sense of competition that was largely absent when most of our offerings to the world were raw materials and cheap staple foodstuffs.

As American production for export continues increasingly toward competitive products, and our productive structure becomes adjusted to an expected substantial volume of foreign sales, the height of the import duties levied by various foreign countries is becoming a matter of more vital concern. A general movement for upward revision of duties has marked the post-war tariff legislation of most countries. This has, in fact, been one of the prime factors in stimulating increasing numbers of American manufacturers to establish assembly plants or branch factories in various foreign countries, as a means of avoiding the higher duties usually levied on the finished products, thus bringing their goods to the foreign consumers at a price that will encourage quantity buying.

SENSITIVENESS OF AMERICAN TRADE AND PROSPERITY TO FOREIGN CONDITIONS

In an increasing number of lines have American producers come to regard foreign sales as part of their regular outlets, as against the attitude of mind some years ago when foreign markets were thought of only sporadically when it was desired to dispose of temporary overstocks. The high productive capacity developed in many lines in this country, beyond the consumptive capacity of the domestic market, is likely to increase the vital interest of American producers in the progress and prosperity of foreign peoples, upon which their purchasing ability for American goods basically rests.

American exporters are likely in the future to be more senstive to the significance of such things as the variations in the size of the coffee crop in Latin America, the price of raw silk in Japan, or the condition of financial stability or the degree of unemployment in the countries of Europe. Whether arising from local conditions of prosperity or depression in those countries, or whether due to the availability of large supplies of competitive products from other sources, the variations in the foreign demand for American export products are likely to have more important repercussions upon domestic prices and prosperity in the United States. In particular commodities, conditions of foreign demand have already come to influence the extent of employment in given industries in the United States, or the acreage to be planted to a given crop.

NEED OF ADJUSTMENT OF SUPPLY AND DEMAND IN WORLD MARKETS

With fast and cheap transportation, and the auxiliary aids of the international telegraph, radio, and telephone services, the world is rapidly becoming contracted into one large market. Under these conditions, the need is likely to become increasingly urgent, not only for full and prompt information as to the conditions of crops, stocks, prices, and requirements all over the world, but for well-laid plans for such control or direction of production in each country that there will be better adjustment of production to demand. It is hardly conceivable that the producers and traders in the various countries will much longer tolerate—without earnest efforts at prevention or at least mitigation—the present unplanned and uncoordinated condition of international markets, that has been resulting in alternate periods of shortage and high prices at one time and overproduction and depressed prices at another. The efforts to attain such a balance of production to market demand, which has been one of the prime objectives of the current movement for international cartels among European producers, may be the forerunner of more extended efforts, in varying forms, towards a better international adjustment of supply and demand. The trend of our foreign trade in recent years gives the United States an increasing stake in such international adjustments.

SUMMARY

Until well into the 19th century, the problem of industry was to produce in sufficient quantity to supply the demand. A general excess of farm products or manufactured goods was largely out of the question. The lack of cheap and adequate transportation facilities between nations was sufficient in itself to prevent the glutting of world markets in staple commodities.

Steam transportation served to break down the barriers in the way of easy communication. A world trade that amounted to less than two billion dollars in 1830 had increased to 68 billions by 1928. Those powers which man had employed in slowly building up a world commerce of 2 billion dollars were suddenly multiplied. This new-found capacity gave rise to a rate of industrial expansion which has resulted in alternate periods of relative shortage and high prices at one time and of overproduction and depressed prices at another.

The year 1830 indicates approximately the time of transition into the new period of rapid industrial acceleration. Staple foodstuffs, minerals and general manufactures were just beginning to enter extensively into international trade. From that period dates the rapid growth into the volume, variety, and breadth of the world commerce we know today.

A review of America's place in world commerce a century ago and now, furnishes a rough measure of the rate of industrial expansion attained. This rate of expansion is a factor of the first importance in charting our future course.

XII

ADVERTISING AND HIGHER STANDARDS OF LIVING

By PAUL H. FASSNACHT

President, Rudolf Mosse, Inc., Berlin, Germany, and New York

EVERY year people in America are acquiring new habits, new tastes and higher standards of living that are tremendously increasing ability to consume. The very inventions, methods and processes that tend to increase production are so increasing the efficiency of man power that the eight-hour day and the five-day week will soon be giving way to a five or six-hour day, possibly a four or even three-day week— with consequent increase in leisure and in opportunity to consume. The working man in the factory, the girl in the shop, today need, want and obtain luxuries that were not available for kings and queens a few decades ago.

The high standards of living in America are the wonder of the world. Advertising has been a most important factor in educating American consumers to this high standard of living. Advertising has enabled manufacturers with sound marketing methods to secure huge volume of sales with amazing rapidity. Processes of growth and development that would have been altogether impossible fifty years ago are now expected as a matter of course by American business executives who have learned to understand and use the power of advertising.

How can this spectacular expansion continue? It is true that competition between manufacturers and advertisers is becoming more and more severe. The million-dollar advertising appropriations of today look back at the hundred-thousand-dollar appropriations of fifteen years ago as mere experiments in advertising. Ten-million-dollar appropriations will be common in 1945 if distribution keeps pace with productive capacity.

This ever-growing competition is constantly sowing seeds of new consumer habits and tastes that will bear fruit in higher standards of living and greater general prosperity providing purchasing power increases in proportion to the expansion in production.

Increase in productive capacity must be offset by a proportionate increase in national income to effect the balance necessary for uninterrupted development and rise in standards of living. Nothing more easily interferes with this balance than uncontrolled rate of expansion of productive capacity. For a time high-pressure advertising and selling and extension of consumer credit through deferred payment plans can solve the problem for individual manufacturers. But consumers cannot long spend more than they earn; if they are to eat more, wear more, travel more and generally consume more they must earn more. And to progressively earn more the consuming millions must have steady employment from employers who are operating at a profit.

Overproduction directly cuts down income. It invariably results in cut-throat price competition, it reduces margins of profit to the vanishing point and until the temporary surplus has disappeared it brings about unemployment and hard times. Nor are the effects of depreciation in a country that is a world power limited to that country. International trade has grown so prodigiously, the commercial relations of the nations of the world have become so close in spite of artificial areas, that any major crisis in the business of a great nation is reflected throughout the world.

The business man today is not only interested in higher standards of living in his own country—rising standards of living throughout the world are his direct concern.

The advertising man who has so materially helped business in its battle to raise standards, create new markets and stimulate prosperity, is likewise interested in the problem internationally. The relation between advertising and standards of living is a direct relation. Advertising men are naturally eager to emphasize the cause-and-effect relation—to point out that advertising has been a potent factor in raising standards of living. They argue, and with conviction, that advertising can and does increase the sum of human wants. They are convinced that the man who has, through advertising, anticipated the thrill of motoring, who has seen pictured in glowing colors the sweeping beauty of the latest super de luxe eight cannot fail to respond with desire. And with the birth of that desire, who can say that that man does not more diligently apply himself to his work, does not make more earnest effort to succeed, to make more money in order that he may possess the motor car of his dreams? Advertising men argue well that advertising is a cause of higher standards of living.

Critics of advertising are often loud in their refusal to believe that advertising has any effect whatever on standards of living. They are quite likely to contend that advertising is a kind of parasitic growth on prosperity, contributing nothing to the business of raising standards of living. These critics are ingenious in their plea that advertising exists *because* of higher standards of living.

But the many ardent defenders of advertising as a constructive force, and the violent few who refuse to believe in its efficacy, nevertheless agree absolutely on one point—that a relation between advertising and standards of living exists.

To be effective, advertising must eventually reach people who have money to spend. In direct measure, the amount of money available for expenditures in home consumption parallels national income. Even casual reference to the following table establishes this point and indicates that in many countries the value of home consumption today actually exceeds the national income.

TABLE I

Country	National Income	Value of Home Consumption
United States	$89,145,000,000	$87,695,000,000
United Kingdom	17,061,000,000	16,358,000,000
Germany	16,344,000,000	16,700,000,000
France	9,418,000,000	9,111,000,000
India	8,251,000,000	8,314,000,000
Canada	5,726,000,000	5,311,000,000
Japan	5,499,000,000	5,566,000,000
Italy	4,480,000,000	4,588,000,000
Australia	2,900,000,000	2,905,000,000
Holland	2,863,000,000	2,788,000,000
Poland	2,243,000,000	2,329,000,000
Czechoslovakia	2,166,000,000	2,101,000,000
Brazil	1,677,000,000	1,654,000,000
Rumania	1,670,000,000	1,639,000,000
Belgium	1,669,000,000	1,619,000,000
Sweden	1,611,000,000	1,602,000,000
Switzerland	1,411,000,000	1,353,000,000
Jugoslavia	1,061,000,000	1,065,000,000
Denmark	954,000,000	954,000,000
Austria	944,000,000	1,055,000,000
Norway	845,000,000	862,000,000
South Africa	755,000,000	697,000,000
Finland	378,000,000	373,000,000
Bulgaria	335,000,000	336,000,000

It is inevitable that the people of no country can long spend more than they earn. National income is the final index to the capacity of peoples of various countries to buy goods and services.

Unless national income increases at least in proportion to the expansion of productive capacity, the fight for markets between individual manufacturers as well as between nations becomes a desperate competition that degenerates rapidly into cut-throat price war. Consequent depression, surplus stocks, unemployment and lowered standards of living cannot and will not support increased advertising budgets. Neither advertising nor any other sales effort can sell goods to people without adequate income.

Throughout the world, therefore, the business man should have the ardent support and enthusiastic cooperation of the advertising man in any battle to overcome a condition that menaces standards of living. Overproduction is a direct challenge to advertising. Without advertising the problem could scarcely exist, because without advertising manufacturers could never have speeded up processes of growth to the danger point.

If, in the past, on occasion advertising men have optimistically counselled expansion with reckless lack of regard for the economics of the client's market, in the future this practice must stop. If, in the past, advertising men have plunged their clients into expansion at home and abroad without proper analysis of consumer's ability to buy, in the future we must see a change in such policies.

Many individual problems of overproduction can be quickly solved by intelligent development of foreign markets. The success of any effort to take up slack, to utilize excess capacity to produce can, however, be made possible by advertising only when the advertising campaign is based upon absolute facts. The successful advertising agency of the future will continue to do more than invent snappy slogans and create pretty pictures. It will be a marketing organization approaching the whole problem of advertising from the economic angle. Business men the world over must inevitably arrive at a satisfactory way to control expansion and to preserve that balance between growth of productive capacity and growth of national income essential to prosperity and rising standards of living. It will increasingly become a primary function of the advertising agency to originate marketing methods and merchandising plans that fully account for all factors involved in problems of stabilization.

XIII

CONSERVATION OF OIL NATIONAL AND INTERNATIONAL PROBLEM

By Sir HENRI DETERDING

Managing Director, Royal Dutch Shell Companies

CONSERVATION of natural resources has generally been regarded as a sacrifice—a benefit conferred on future generations. It is more than that. In the oil industry at least conservation is the only way to eliminate the evils of overproduction; the only sensible way to bring order out of chaos.

Without conservation the industry will continue to bring in new producing fields before they are needed; price wars will continue; oil profits will disappear. According to E. B. Reeser, President of the American Petroleum Institute, the oil industry in the United States has not earned more than 3½ per cent on its total investment for a number of years. In 1927 the return was less than 1 per cent. Nor is this condition peculiar to the United States. In many sections of the world today it is not paying the big companies to produce oil.

Overproduction encourages wasteful producers to multiply at the expense of those which have a larger amount of capital tied up in plant equipment and reserves; in adequate research and technical staffs. The efficient producer cannot afford to operate exclusively for immediate profits. The future for stockholders and employees, for depreciation and depletion charges, must be considered. Further, if the United States or any other nation is to safeguard itself against ultimate failure of its domes-

tic supply, the oil leaders in the industry must encourage fore-
thought and conservation of capital resources.

There are wise men of distinction who have been saying,
Is the United States going on producing all it can, and more
than it can consume, with the result that it is exporting today
at a low price what it is likely to be importing later on at a higher
price? Is it going on overproducing today when it may be over-
consuming in a few years?

The point has not been put which is in many minds outside of the States, and that is: Are we, the public outside the
United States, going to rely on supplies from that country
when these may be less at some approaching time, seeing that
no thought is given to conservation?

That of late years American producers have taken an interest, and more than a passing one, in foreign producing fields
is really the outcome of the sound view that the world should
ńot be entirely dependent on one country of supply.

But then why not go a step further on this international
way and preserve the supply of your own country for the time
when you do not want to export it, but can realize for it the
price which it would cost others to bring it to its destination
in the States?

What is to be done? What is the best thing to do for the
industry as a whole?

Well, first of all, conservation. Let us gradually, practically
and scientifically realize what we have got and how we can
draw on it liberally, not only now but in the future—that is,
if we come to the conclusion that we continue to export the
excess over consumption, to see in how far such excess is going
to be lasting.

Under existing conditions the exports from America are
simply looked upon as temporary dumping of excess production. This practice has far-reaching results. It leads an undue
amount of American oil to find its way to India, or Persian

oil to Iceland. The consuming areas and producing areas of the world are thrown out of balance. According to the best authorities, the oil resources of the United States constitute only 18 per cent of the world total. And they are being drawn upon several times faster than the rest of the world's resources. America is producing 68.9 per cent of the world's crude oil.

Physical waste caused by overproduction has been very great. While progress has been made in the elimination of this form of waste it apparently still persists, however. Dr. George Otis Smith recently described a well that was brought in in California at the rate of 3500 barrels a day. At the same time it was discharging 75,000,000 cubic feet of gas a day—more than enough gas to supply the city of San Francisco. For every dollar of oil produced more than a dollar of gas was wasted. According to Mr. W. Alton Jones, chairman of the Executive Committee of Henry L. Doherty & Company, "Last year there were approximately 22,000 wells drilled in this country in the search for oil. Of this number one-half produced gas in varying quantities and in untold instances much of this gas was blown in the air and all or a part of it wasted or used very uneconomically."

Under the leasing and royalty practices of the United States it is almost impossible to conserve oil underground. In favoring the lessor, competition forces new fields into use even though there is more than enough oil on the market to meet the demand. The lessee is usually required, under the terms of the lease, to start drilling to protect the property from drainage by offset wells.

Due very often to divided ownership and small areas, the drainage of which is threatened by adjacent wells, a rush of drilling leads to flush flows which temporarily glut the market. In order to secure proper drainage and conserve lifting power of the gas, wells should not average more than one for every 9 or 10 acres. Very often there is a well to each acre.

President Hoover and the Department of the Interior advise the unit development of oil fields, with a view to sinking wells only where necessary. Under these conditions oil would not be produced until provision had been made for utilizing the gas, and there was a proper market for the gas and oil. The proceeds would be divided among the owners in proportion to their holdings. The idea seems to have made considerable progress in California.

The Petroleum Institute has drawn up a national code of marketing practices for refining petroleum products. It has endorsed the enactment of laws to permit agreements between operators in a single pool for orderly development of oil and gas holdings. It has sanctioned investment in public authority of power to prevent continuance of drilling practices which result in underground physical waste of oil and gas. It has pledged cooperation with the Federal Oil Conservation Board and with the United States Bureau of Public Roads and State Highways in a comprehensive program of cooperation and conservation of oil resources.

This program ran foul of "restraint of trade" technicalities. The Federal Oil Conservation Board, the American Petroleum Institute, and the American Bar Association suggested that the Sherman Law could be overcome through inter-oil state agreements. In the minds of many there seems to be considerable doubt as to whether this would provide a permanent solution of the overproduction problem.

It looks very much as if the American people would have to dig further down, if they are determined to bring the anti-trust laws into conformity with a program of conservation. Such a program would apply to all industries because the oil industry is not alone subject to overproduction. Possibly all industries and all nations are faced with the task of reinterpreting the term "conservation."

We are living in the age of cooperation, not only as the

man of the street thinks of it, but in the sense of a very much higher cooperative vein—an aim based on the fact that all industries are becoming visibly (as they always have been logically but too silently) interdependent.

Let us realize that where there are several dozens of large producers and marketers and joint action is necessary the individual should sink vanity and should aim at continually sound business rather than at temporarily being "a big oil man" with its big burdens and responsibilities.

XIV

THE WASTES RESULTING FROM BUSINESS OPERATIONS TOO SMALL IN SCALE

By PAUL T. CHERINGTON

Director of Research, J. Walter Thompson Company

In this country most of the discussion of operating scale in recent years has been concerned with the dangers of operating business on too big a scale. These dangers, in the main, have been of two types: the social dangers arising from monopoly, and the dangers of incompetence arising from inadequate management or inefficient operation.

There is a department of American business, however, which has developed within itself, almost without notice from economists and sociologists, a set of high social costs and economic dangers arising out of operation on too small a scale.

In production the problem of the optimum scale is present, but usually in the form of a danger that the plant will get too big to be well managed. In wholesale distribution good management is easier to find than a really competent line organization. But in retail distributing operations the real menace is the danger of allowing the business to be too small to pay the going rate for managerial brains out of the normal mark-up.

When we have a Census of Distribution (or better, when we have had several to compare), we shall be much more certain in our interpretation (even in our recognition) of these controlling factors than we are now. How this will be apt to work out may be gathered from some points developed in the trial census made in eleven cities a year or more ago and their bearing on certain matters which now seem remote, but which may shape the future of the retail end of distribution. This preliminary census seems to shed light on two facts which are of the sort likely to determine the retail forms and methods of the future.

These two facts are:

1. It is doubtful whether a one-man shop is a distributing operation which society can afford to support, as its only retail resource.

2. It may be that independence, as now understood, and as applied to the small retailer, is for him an extravagant and undesirable luxury.

The prevailing opinion has been that it was big business which was looting the poor consumer. Now the idea seems to be penetrating slowly that in many ways the draft on the public imposed by big business is a mere bagatelle compared with the cost of trying to distribute merchandise through concerns too small to be operated competently. The predatory trust now is sharing the limelight with the parasitic incompetent.

THE PARASITIC SMALL DEALER

When railroads first began to be built, capital was shy and ideas were small. All the early railroads were short lines and their operating organizations and finances were correspondingly small. One man could, and sometimes did, own a whole line and he controlled labor, rates, and services to suit himself. To make a long story short it has been found that a railroad built and operated on that scale is too small. The independence of such a miniature magnate was too costly a luxury to be supported by the small territory served. We have still to find just the combination of large and small scale elements which is best in railroad operation. We do not yet know whether we want 3 or 5 or 7 trunk lines; but we do know that we don't want a hundred, and we know that we don't want to transfer freight or change cars ten times between here and Chicago. Similarly in the case of telephones, oil refineries, steel rolling mills, and other enterprises the continuous search for the optimum scale has led into larger operating units.

These familiar parallels should be kept in mind in connection with our thoughts about merchandise distribution. Chain stores and department stores have some economic sins to answer for, but perhaps we can get a better idea of their real place in the scheme of things if we think of them as an experiment in a new operating scale, rather than as the enemy of a perfect form of independent merchant who had attained a demonstrable perfection in service and economy in cost.

Look at this table, for example, giving the results in percentages of an actual store-to-store census of over 95,000 retailers in the eleven city census:

| | Per Cent of Total | | | |
| | Belonging to Chains | | Independent | |
	Number of Stores	Total Sales	Number of Stores	Total Sales
All stores................	15.1	28.7	84.9	71.3
Gas and oil stations.........	46.4	73.5	53.6	26.5
Hats and caps—men's......	33.7	51.7	66.3	48.3
Boot and shoe.............	27.3	51.8	72.7	48.2
Grocery and delicatessen....	21.0	41.3	79.0	58.7
Drugs...................	11.8	29.9	88.2	70.1

Chain stores figured to some extent in every one of the 40 trades reported on. Even the custom tailor business reported nearly 2 per cent of the stores and over 11 per cent of the business being in chain store companies and the motorcycle and bicycle shops—the very last stand of the independent—showed 3.4 per cent of the shops and 4.5 per cent of the business to have abandoned its independence and gone into chain control.

If the chain store is a disease it is an alarmingly prevalent one. If it carries a threat to the existence of the independent retailer, then the independent is in a very bad fix. But if it is an intelligent experiment in finding more efficient scales for ownership, financing, and operation of retail establishments, than the one-man store proved to be, then it is a thing to be watched with interest and tested in economic cold blood.

One important phase of this matter of operating scale for retailers is the question whether society could afford to keep on with the old independent form of store as its sole dependence in merchandise distribution, even if that were likely to happen. The same census shows that in the eleven cities there was a grocery or a delicatessen store for every 325 people. In other words 60 consumer families, more or less, supported one of these stores. Now, if each of these groceries were the source of livelihood for a grocer and his family, it would mean that each of these 60 consumer families was the sole support of a grocer and his family for five days in every year. Or, to make it more graphic still, if the grocer were boarded around, like the old-time school teacher, each family would have the grocer and his tribe quartered on them for free board and lodging five days a year.

That wouldn't be so bad if the grocer were alone, but the confectioner and the meat men would follow him for two days each, and the druggist for a day, the restaurant keeper for a three days' change from his own providings, and a flock of other retailers for various lengths of time. Put in this way, the social cost of maintaining a score of independent shops to do the work of one, becomes clear.

INCOMPETENT RETAILING TOO COSTLY FOR THE RETAILER

But the cost to society of an inefficient scale is only one part of the story. What about its cost to the retailer himself? If these small-scale retailers were getting rich out of the process then they would be small-scale pirates just like any other predatory villains; but if they are taxing society unduly and are not getting even a decent living out of it, then they are not robbers to be caught and locked up; they are plain incompetents to be put out of their economic misery as speedily and effectually as possible. As one small store-keeper recently put it: "I must either get more business, or get a higher price, or I must go to work."

Here are some more figures from the Distribution Census

| | Per Cent of Independent Stores | | | | | |
| | Total Sales Below $5000 | | Total Sales Below $50,000 | | Total Sales Above $50,000 | |
	No. of Stores	Total Sales	No. of Stores	Total Sales	No. of Stores	Total Sales
All stores..................	28.06	1.68	88.66	29.47	11.34	70.53
Boot and shoe..............	26.64	1.83	87.52	40.90	12.48	59.10
Men's clothing.............	20.00	1.01	81.53	24.82	18.47	75.16
Women's clothing..........	19.92	0.62	71.88	12.41	28.12	87.59
Drug stores................	8.15	0.62	89.83	65.22	10.17	34.78
Dry goods and notions.......	30.92	2.62	91.75	38.97	8.25	61.03
Electrical appliances.........	28.13	1.55	80.55	30.14	19.45	69.86
Fruit and vegetables.........	35.08	5.92	95.91	70.37	4.09	29.63
Furniture..................	28.44	1.13	76.97	16.92	23.03	83.08
Groceries and delicatessen....	27.42	3.96	94.34	67.68	5.66	32.32
Hardware..................	19.85	1.43	85.60	34.34	14.40	65.68
Meat, poultry, fish..........	11.64	1.06	88.28	55.55	11.72	44.45
Plumbing..................	24.23	1.27	26.70	22.88	23.30	77.12

(Of the department stores 93.52 per cent reported more than $100,000 sales and these did 99 per cent of the total department store business.)

in eleven cities——figures covering the 80,000 independent retail stores.

The picture presented by this table has two sides. We have been so frightened by the fact that 12 per cent of the stores did 70 per cent of the business (with all the implications of monopoly that fact involves), that we have not been shocked enough by the other equally significant facts that there were 28 per cent of the stores trying to make a living out of 1.6 per cent of the business sold less than $50,000 worth of goods a year, each.

Before we take up the meaning of this to the individual merchant just look down the third column in the table and see how many of the stores in various lines of business were under the $50,000 line—they range from 71 to 95 per cent.

Now, of course, nobody would argue that all stores doing less than $50,000 a year should be closed, but we still lack a sufficiently clear idea of the economic cost of small-scale retail operation, from the standpoint of the retailer under present day conditions.

The fundamental difficulty with small-scale retailing is the fact that the price of human brains of the type necessary for conducting a retail establishment has risen substantially during the past few years. Practically all the skilled trades and crafts, by collective bargaining, have been able to get from society an increased return for their labor. This, of course, not only is desirable from a social point of view; it is one reason for the great expansion of our markets for consumer goods. (The retailer storekeeper who, in a sense, sells his brains in competition with these skilled crafts, cannot by unionizing, raise his compensation from society because that compensation does not come in the form of a wage, but in the form of a net profit on merchandise sold—mark-up times turnover, minus cost of doing business.)   And these consumers, with enlarged incomes, do not feel disposed to give up their expanded wages in needlessly large merchant profits.

It is difficult for any retail business to count consistently on more than about 2.1 per cent net profit. This means that unless a retail business can make more than $50,000 worth of sales in a year its proprietor cannot count on a weekly profit of much over $23.00. This is less than the market price for good brains of the necessary type. This plain statement is not an argument on either side of a controversial question. It is plain arithmetic.

Of course, lots of independent merchants are willing to do business for less than $23.00 a week net profit, rather than "go to work." But the cost to them, and to society, of their continuing to operate below the minimum scale for competent retailing is one phase of the economics of merchandise distribution which has been neglected.

It is not the chain store, or the department store, or the mail order house, but it is the irresistible and remorseless final consumer, who is, in effect, saying to the small merchant:

Why should we keep on maintaining you in what you choose to call "independent" operation on an incompetent basis? Is it asking too much to insist that you either become competent or go to work at something else?

The monopoly dangers in any large scale of retail enterprise so far developed are negligible compared with the huge, continuous, and futile cost of retail operation on a wastefully and incompetently small scale. We ought to be really worried about the high cost of independence, so long as that independence implies incompetent operating practices or wasteful operating scale.

One other important aspect of this problem is developed by an examination of some of the figures for the independent retailers who are making an apparent success of retailing. Evidently, the problem is being solved by the public in its own way, by giving its business to those who have demonstrated their ability to serve economically. Leaving the chain stores out of consideration, for the present, the facts from the eleven city censuses about independent stores doing more than $100,000 worth of business a year each make it clear that, perhaps unconsciously, the public, in many lines of business already is giving its patronage to the larger units. In 19 trades over half of the business now is in the hands of the big stores, and in all but 8 the share of the big stores is over 25 per cent. In these eight trades ranking lowest in this respect the big stores were uniformly less than 3 per cent of the total number.

It may be that the small independent merchant is destined to follow the hand-weaver, the county telephone, and the ten-mile railroad. If he is, the public will get its compensation for the loss of his independence by being better served; and he will be obliged to get his by taking advantage of the bettered status of the "hired man."

XV

THE GROWTH OF INDUSTRIAL AND FINANCIAL UNITS

By FRANCIS H. SISSON

Vice-President, Guaranty Trust Company of New York

No single economic movement of the present day is more universal in its manifestations or more significant in its bearing on the industrial future than the increasing tendency toward the national and international domination of industry and finance by syndicates of great wealth and power. This tendency has been visible for many years—has, in fact, developed as a necessary corollary of the Industrial Revolution. It has taken innumerable forms and has encountered many obstacles and many setbacks, both economic and political; but, in general, it has swept on with irresistible and ever-increasing force, until it has become evident that the typical business enterprise of the future will be built on the foundation of mass production and mass distribution. How far the movement will ultimately go, and what economic, social, and political changes it may bring in its wake, can only be imagined. But its essential soundness has been amply demonstrated. It has not only brought increased profits to owners of shares, but has also paid higher wages to workers and placed better products on the market at lower prices. In this way it has served seemingly conflicting interests by achieving greater operating efficiency and by dividing the benefits among the various groups concerned.

Whatever may prove to be the ultimate limits of this process of integration, they have not yet appeared. So far as has yet been demonstrated, the benefits to be derived from large-scale methods increase with the growth of the enterprise or association. Beyond a certain point, the purely physical advantages of machine operation and division of labor cease to be significant. But, long before this point is reached, other benefits become apparent. The company assumes, in a constantly increasing degree, the nature of a public institution. There are two main reasons for this development. The first is the recognition that the abuse of power must bring its inevitable penalty in the form of public regulation or possible suppression. The second is the fact that the direction of affairs on such a vast scale naturally passes into the hands of high-grade men who, entirely aside from the danger of political interference, realize that their interests and those of their stockholders are best served, in the long run, by a steady and healthy growth based on the principles of fair dealing. A new expression, "business statesmanship," has come to be applied to the broader and more intelligent way in which industrial and financial leaders now recognize their public responsibilities.

It has already been said that the growth of large-scale business units has occurred as a consequence and a necessary accompaniment of the Industrial Revolution. Prior to the modern era of factory production, there were isolated examples of great business enterprises; but these were mainly artificial monopolies created and protected by political power. In the main, production and distribution were carried on by individuals and partnerships operating on a small scale until the remarkable series of mechanical discoveries and inventions about 150 years ago gave rise to the modern movement.

For many years, the process of growth was relatively slow. With occasional exceptions, business enterprises continued to operate locally and in competition with numerous other enterprises of approximately equal size. Where large concerns existed, their operations were based mainly on the technical advantages of large-scale machine production. It was less than fifty years ago that the realization of the gains to be derived from an elimination of competition began to find expression in the formation of consolidations, trusts, and cartels.

Curiously enough, only one year elapsed between the formation of the Standard Oil Company, the first great American combination, and the International Rail Makers' Association, the earliest of the important European international cartels. The Standard Oil Company was formed in 1882, and for five years existed as the only organization of its kind in the United States. In 1887, the American Sugar Refining Company was established, an organization that is usually regarded as marking the beginning of the "trust movement" in this country. Although neither the number nor the magnitude of the combinations formed in these early years gave any indication of assuming a major importance, public suspicion was quickly aroused. Even before the passage of the Sherman Act in 1890, numerous States had passed anti-trust laws. Nevertheless, several other combinations were formed before the panic of 1893 temporarily brought the movement to a halt. Among these were the National Lead Company, the Distilling and Cattle-Feeding Trusts, the American Tobacco Company, the General Electric Company, and the United States Rubber Company. Altogether, about twenty combinations had listed their securities on the New York Stock Exchange by 1893, the total capital stock of all these companies being somewhat less than one billion dollars.

The movement recommenced on a large scale in 1898, and gained momentum so rapidly that in the three years from 1897 to 1900, inclusive, no less than 149 important consolidations, involving a total capitalization of $3,578,650,000, took place. Hardly an important industry was unrepresented in this list. Coal-mining, iron and steel, copper, lead, zinc, silver, paper, leather, rubber, salt, starch, chemicals, cordage, ice, glass, paving, and roofing, and other branches of basic manufacture were drastically affected, and in many cases entirely reorganized by consolidation. In the field of consumer's goods, this period witnessed the formation of such historic organizations as the re-formed Standard Oil Company, the United Fruit Company, the National Biscuit Company, the Diamond Match Company, the American Woolen Company, the International Thread Company, the American Writing-Paper Company, the United States Flour-Milling Company, the International Silver Company, the American Bicycle Company, and the American Chicle Company.

Although these early consolidations were by no means uniformly successful, their experience in general was such that the movement grew steadily. A committee of Congress in 1913 enumerated 200 consolidations with some degree of monopolistic control. The trend is shown by the increase in the average size of manufacturing establishments, as reported in the United States Census of Manufactures. The average capital of manufacturing plants in this country in 1899 was only $43,250. By 1904 it had increased to $58,600; by 1909, to $68,600; and by 1914, to $82,600. In the latter year, the average capital of establishments with an annual output aggregating $5,000 or more in value was about $128,600; by 1919 this figure had increased to $206,750. This comparison, however, must take account of the great increase in average prices during the war. A recent study of mergers by Professor Willard L. Thorpe shows that the number increased from 89 in 1919 to 207 in 1927, and the number of companies merged from 292 to 678. The number of manufacturing establishments reported by the Census of Manufactures as having an annual product valued at $5,000 or more was 177,110 in 1914, 214,383, in 1919, and only 191,866 in 1927. The value of the products of these establishments increased from less than $24,000,000,000 in 1914 to $62,000,000,000 in 1919 and $62,721,-

000,000 in 1927, despite the decline in the price level during the latter period. The value of the product of the average establishment, therefore, amounted to $326,900 in 1927, as compared with $289,400 in 1919 and $135,400 in 1914. An allowance for changes in the price level would show a less rapid gain in the first half of the period and a more rapid gain in the second half.

This comparison, however, fails to show the whole picture, since the "establishment," as reported by the Bureau of the Census, signifies, in most cases, a single plant or manufacturing unit. In some cases, where the ownership and management are unified and only one set of books is kept, two or more plants are considered a single establishment. But the number of establishments in this enumeration is certainly much greater than the number of organizations represented in their ownership and control. Many of our leading industrial corporations operate, either directly or through subsidiaries, a large number of plants scattered throughout the country.

A brief review of the leading American industries serves to indicate the extent to which great combinations of capital have come to occupy commanding positions in our economic system. In the iron and steel industry, we have an outstanding example in the United States Steel Corporation; in the automobile industry, General Motors; in the electrical equipment industry, the General Electric Company; in telephone communication, the American Telephone and Telegraph Company; in agricultural implements, the International Harvester Company; in rubber goods, the United States Rubber Company; in meat packing, Swift and Armour; in petroleum, the Standard Oil group; in other manufacturing lines, such organizations as duPont and the Radio Corporation; and in retail merchandising, Sears Roebuck, Atlantic and Pacific, Woolworth, and others. This list might be extended to many times its length and still include only comparatively few of the great industrial combinations operating in the United States today.

Remarkable as this development is, it is in some respects less striking than the similar movement that has been taking place in Europe. This fact is due in some measure to the suspicious and antagonistic attitude that has prevailed in the United States toward the "trusts" during the greater part of their history. In view of the professed motives and the general attitude of some of the early American industrial combinations, this hostility on the part of the public is not difficult to understand. The merger movement had made very little progress before it was checked by the enactment of Federal and State statutes designed to prevent the formation of monopolies. The Sherman Act, passed in 1890, declared "every contract, combination in the form of trust or otherwise, or conspiracy in restraint of trade of commerce" illegal, and provided that "every person who shall monopolize, or attempt to monopolize, or combine or conspire with any other person or persons, to monopolize any part of the trade or commerce among the several states, or with foreign countries, shall be deemed guilty of a misdemeanor." This act still constitutes the backbone of the policy of the Federal Government toward industrial combinations. The wide opportunity for interpretation which it presents has, however, made it the subject of many court decisions; and both these decisions and the methods adopted for its enforcement have reflected the changes that have gradually come about in the general attitude of the public toward "big business."

At present it is held that, under the Sherman Law, competing business enterprises may merge or otherwise combine, provided that the combination is warranted by sound economic considerations, and provided that there remain outside of the merger enough competing concerns of sufficient strength to ensure the continuance of active competition at virtually every point throughout the industry. The tendency in recent years has been for the Federal Trade Commission, the Department of Justice, and the courts to construe the law in an increasingly broad and liberal way. The trend is unmistakably shown by the fact that there has been no court decision under the Federal anti-trust laws in the last five years.

The same trend toward consolidation is apparent in other branches of economic activity, no less clearly than in manufacture. One of the most striking developments in recent years has been the phenomenal growth of the "chain store" in the field of retail merchandising. It is estimated that more than 15 per cent of all retail business in the United States is now handled by chain stores, and the proportion is steadily increasing.

In the railroad and public-utility fields, the growth in the relative size of the individual unit is equally striking, although the nature of the functions performed by these companies has directed the movement along somewhat different lines. Among the railroads, a certain amount of competition has always existed; and in the past the rivalry between roads serving the same territory has frequently led to most unfortunate results. Although the present railroad policy of the United States Government, as defined in the Transportation Act of 1920, contemplates a limited amount of competition under strict regulation, the idea that a free competitive market for transportation service is either possible or desirable has long since been abandoned. Many voluntary railroad consolidations have taken place in the past; and, while the movement has been interrupted in recent years by the refusal of the Interstate Commerce Commission to permit mergers in the absence of a definite nation-wide consolidation program, as contemplated by the Transportation Act, both the provisions of the law and the policy of railroad officials indicate that the trend toward centralization of control has only been temporarily checked. The announcement by the Interstate Commerce Commission of its tentative consolidation plan at the end of 1929 has already been followed by one major consolidation in line with its provisions. The plan is, however, admittedly tentative and subject to modification; and the final formulation and execution of a complete consolidation program will be a long process that may necessitate further legislation.

For many years the element of competition has been almost entirely absent in public-utility operation. Telephone and telegraph service has become concentrated in the hands of a few large companies operating on a nation-wide or a world-wide scale. Electric traction has usually been carried on as a local monopoly, although this branch of public service has been forced to meet severe competition from automotive transportation in recent years. The production of gas and electricity under competitive conditions involves such enormous wastes in duplication of equipment that local monopoly is almost universal. The consolidation movement in the public-utility field has, therefore, taken the form of financial integration through the acquisition of control of local operating companies by holding companies. The purpose of such consolidations is to increase earnings through more efficient and economical methods of operation and to reduce interest charges by the distribution of risk. Endeavor along this line has been so successful that the movement has swept over the entire country, until now a large proportion of the local producers of gas and electricity are under the control of holding companies.

A somewhat similar motive underlies the formation of investment trusts, or companies organized to hold the securities of other companies. This is another form of integration that has gained enormous headway in this country in the last few years. Essentially, the investment trust is an intermediary between the individual investor and the operating company. It may be termed a sort of investment insurance. However, the fact that the ownership of corporate shares carries with it a voice in the management of industry gives the investment trust a position that approaches, by imperceptible degrees, that of a holding company. Partly for this reason, the question of regulation of investment trusts has become an important one; and, if this type of organization continues to expand as rapidly in the future as it has in the recent past, the problem will certainly increase in magnitude and complexity.

The unification of control over certain industrial functions through the formation of trade associations is another important aspect of the movement toward centralization. Instead of representing a complete merging of interests among two or more companies, the trade association leaves each company in the industry to maintain its own identity and, in general, to manage its own affairs. The association concerns itself with the performance of some particular function in which a need for cooperative action has become apparent. In performing this function, however, it ordinarily enlists the aid of a large number of individual enterprises—in many cases, practically every important firm in the industry is a member. Here, again, the benefits to be gained through united action have become so apparent that the number and size of trade associations have increased very rapidly, imposing new problems of regulation on State and Federal boards.

Mergers, acquisitions of control, and trade agreements are not, however, the only ways in which our modern industrial giants have developed. Many cases could be cited of companies that have grown to enormous proportions without resorting to consolidation in any form. An outstanding example of this type of organization is the Ford Motor Company. Even in numerous instances where consolidation has taken place, one or both of the parties have been companies that had already gained a preeminent position in their industry under purely competitive conditions.

The movement toward centralization is also apparent among the banks. The series of large banking consolidations in the last few years represents an effort on the part of financial institutions to keep pace with their industrial clients. Such development is necessary if the banks are to continue to serve the needs of industry and commerce in the future as successfully as they have in the past. It is neither legal nor in accord with sound banking practice for a bank to lend an unduly large proportion of its funds to any single individual or corporation. Consequently, the bank's facilities must expand along with the needs of its clients.

It has already been pointed out that the movement toward centralization has, in some respects, made more progress in Europe than in the United States. In general, the trend has been less toward the merging of companies and more toward the formation of trade associations or, as they are usually termed, cartels. And the proximity of the European countries to one another has naturally brought about a more extensive international movement than has taken place in this country.

The earliest of the great European cartels was the International Rail Makers' Association, commonly known as "Irma." This trust was organized in England in 1883, and included British, German, and Belgian rail producers. Dissatisfaction over production quotas led to its dissolution in 1886; and it was not revived until 1904, when France joined. The agreement was for a term of three years, and in 1907 it was not renewed. In 1912 another three-year agreement was drawn up, American producers being among the members. In this instance the life of the cartel was cut short by the outbreak of the World War. It was not re-formed until 1926, when it became the European Rail Makers' Association, American producers refusing to join because of their uncertainty as to its status under the anti-trust laws of the United States.

The formation of this association was quickly followed by

similar agreements in other industries. No less than forty industries are known to have been involved in such agreements in 1897. By the time the World War broke out, 114 recognized international cartels were in existence, including 26 in coal, iron, steel, and other metals; 19 in chemical and allied industries; 18 in transportation, mainly shipping; 15 in textiles; 8 in stoneware and porcelain; 7 in paper and pulp; 6 in stones and earth; 5 in electrical equipment; and 10 in miscellaneous industries.

Since the end of the war, the formation of cartels has proceeded very rapidly, partly because of the impaired purchasing power of European countries in general and the consequent necessity of limiting output, and partly because of the desire of European producers to increase their competitive strength in foreign markets in order to meet American competition. Among the most important of these recent agreements are the International Incandescent Lamp Cartel, formed in 1925; the Association of Glue Manufacturers, organized a year later; Copper Exporters, Inc., which came into existence at about the same time; a zinc cartel established by German, Belgian, and English firms; an international association of producers of superphosphates in seventeen countries, including the United States; a European aluminum cartel; renewals of former agreements among cement producers; an association of magnesia producers in five countries; the potash agreement among German and French producers; and, most important of all, the International Steel Convention, representing "the restoration of the interaction between the heavy industry of Western Germany and that of the adjacent States, which depend so inextricably upon one another."

A number of international combines or trusts have united to form cartels, which in some instances occupy a position approaching monopoly. The earliest important movements in this direction took place in the production of explosives, petroleum, and electrical equipment. There have been numerous other attempts from time to time to gain world-wide monopolistic control over some basic commodity, a notable example being the effort of French and American interests to "corner" copper about thirty years ago. No such attempt has ever succeeded. In a few cases, national monopolies have existed in certain lines; occasionally such monopolies are protected by government concessions. But in general, the experience of European as well as American companies and associations indicates that "horizontal combinations," formed for the purpose of gaining monopolistic control over any branch of industry, tend to break down under their own weight. Some of the most conspicuous successes have been achieved by the "vertical combinations," such as the United States Steel Corporation, which are based on the coordination of effort in the various stages of production, from the raw material to the finished product.

Nevertheless, there is no mistaking the signs of the times. Concentration of control, whether of the "vertical" or the "horizontal" type, is the order of the day. Statistics are cited to show that merged companies have not been conspicuously more successful in the past than those that have not merged. The essential distinction, however, is not between merged and unmerged companies, but between large and small business units, regardless of the circumstances of their origin. And there can be no doubt as to the present relative position of the typical large concern as contrasted with that of the small one. Earnings of the leading corporations in this country last year were the largest on record; while, on the other hand, business failures were the most numerous, and the average liabilities of bankrupt concerns the smallest, in many years. These facts indicate very strongly that, in a general way, the great corporations are gaining at the expense of the small producers and distributors.

It would be a great mistake, however, to conclude that this tendency implies a corresponding concentration of ultimate ownership in industrial and commercial enterprises. The reverse is true. Both directly and indirectly, the general public is increasing its financial stake in the future of industry. Not only are the employees and customers of industrial and public service corporations becoming part owners of these corporations; but through the insurance companies and the savings banks they are rapidly increasing what may be termed their indirect ownership. In this way the lines formerly drawn between labor, capital, and the consumer are becoming blurred and indistinct. Although it would be easy to exaggerate the extent and the immediate possibilities of this movement, there can be no doubt that the tendency is highly significant, and that it must be borne in mind in any consideration of the true meaning of industrial centralization.

This diffusion of ownership undoubtedly offers a partial explanation of the change in the attitude of the public toward "big business" during the last thirty years. For the rest, there has been a complete reversal of policy on the part of business itself, along with a most convincing demonstration of the fact that centralization of control makes for economy of industrial effort. Thirty years ago, the "trusts" were frankly predatory; they were organized and conducted by a few wealthy "captains of industry" for their own personal gain; and free competition was regarded by the public at large as the panacea for all economic ills. This was the atmosphere out of which the Sherman Law arose. While it is true that some such restriction was imperatively necessary at that time, it is equally true that the makers of the Sherman Law, in endeavoring to correct certain evils, inadvertently placed a stumbling-block in the path of economic progress. Like many other laws of its kind, it went too far. Now that the public and the government have learned to welcome and foster, rather than fear, the general tendency toward consolidation, the Sherman Law is recognized as an obsolescent, if not obsolete, statute, enacted in an effort to legislate out of existence certain fundamental economic laws. The ingenuity of business leaders has been taxed to find methods whereby the sound development of their companies might be furthered without violating the law, while the government and the courts have been forced to shape their policies of administration and construction to conform with the changes of public opinion. ,

The economic forces behind the consolidation movement are irresistible; and the results already achieved are sufficient to demonstrate that the advantages of free competition, from the point of view of the people as a whole, are immeasurably out-weighed by those of cooperation. Different branches of economic effort profit from unification in different ways and in different degrees; in some lines the urge is much stronger than in others. But, in one way or another, industry, commerce, transportation, communication, finance, and even agriculture are following the universal trend. In manufacturing, the chief considerations are in the handling of material, the use of machinery and departments, the division and sub-division of labor, the vertical integration of successive processes, the making and marketing of by-products, the division of functions among different plants, and the expenditure of large sums of money on research. Other advantages, which may be termed business advantages, are almost universal in their application. These include large-scale buying and selling, the distribution and stabilization of activity among different operating units, the more effective use of advertising and selling methods, the lower cost of capital, high-grade management, the regulation of output, and the elimination of the abuses that almost invariably arise under conditions of severe competition.

Needless to say, the trend toward business integration imposes new problems, both on business leaders and on governmental agencies. It can be achieved only through the sacrifice of the automatic regulation that free competition has always provided. For this automatic regulation must be substituted an artificial regulation dependent on human wisdom and foresight, and subject to the weaknesses of human nature. For such a system to operate successfully, it is imperative that both business and political ethics be raised to a higher level than has been maintained in the past. Fortunately, there are indications that this necessity is being recognized, and that a new code of business ethics, at least, is being developed along with the growth of business units.

Any attempt to measure the progress of the consolidation movement by statistical means is a well-nigh hopeless task, honeycombed as modern business is with combines, semi-monopolies, holding companies, interlocking directorates, trade associations, and "gentlemen's agreements." The enormous strides that have been made in recent years, can, however, be realized to some extent by a comparison of the present with the not-distant past. At the beginning of the present century there were probably less than two hundred consolidated companies of large size operating in the United States, and the combined capitalization of these concerns did not exceed five billion dollars. Today, the Standard Oil group alone has a paid-up capital of more than four billions. If we add to this the capital and surplus of one agricultural machinery company, one automobile company, one rubber company, two chemical companies, one coal company, three copper companies, two electrical goods companies, one baking company, one sewing-machine company, one shoe machinery company, two meat-packing companies, two non-ferrous metal companies other than copper, one railway equipment, one paper company, three chain-store companies, two mail-order houses, two steel companies, one sugar refining company, three tobacco companies, eleven public-utility holding companies, six gas and electric companies, two telephone and telegraph companies, one woolen goods company, and three miscellaneous manufacturing companies—only eighty-seven companies in all—we have a total of more than $16,500,000,000. This list hardly scratches the surface, even in the United States; it includes none of the large "independent" oil companies; it includes no trade associations; and it includes no foreign companies or cartels.

The age of "big business" is here to stay. Our problem is not to hinder its development, but to promote it and direct it in such a way as to reap its full benefits without suffering from its possible evils.

XVI

OVERPRODUCTION AND BUSINESS ORGANIZATION

By Dr. VIRGIL JORDAN

Economist, McGraw-Hill Publishing Company

OVERPRODUCTION IS a feature of present-day business easy enough to observe, but very difficult to understand. Its effects are evident in unemployment and lowered profits, but its causes are complex and deeply hidden in the structure of our business and financial organization. It is hard to see why anybody should suffer from having too much in a world where a good deal of want is found everywhere at all times. But in this society in which serving human needs is still secondary and incidental to making money, feast and famine are constant companions, or always close on each other's heels.

It has probably always been so. In no society we know of, and at no period in history, has the supply of the necessaries of life and of other human wants been made available to everyone smoothly and regularly for any length of time without a hitch. Yet the reasons why the system of supplying men's needs has broken down more or less inevitably, if not periodically, have differed greatly from one period of history or one stage of economic organization to another. Natural causes—crop failures due to weather, storms; earthquakes, pestilences, as well as wars and revolutions, of course, have always operated, and still do, to disturb the functioning of the economic system. But it is the defects in the system itself that are most important, because we think they are most susceptible of control; and it is hard to say whether in that respect matters have improved in the course of the long evolution of economic organization. If it were not for the natural or circumstantial factors just mentioned, it is probable that the system of small agricultural holdings and of small scale, even handcraft manufacture, which existed between the breakdown of feudalism and the advent of the industrial revolution might be considered the most stable of all the forms of economic organization that have developed, although it did not supply as high a standard of living for parts of the population as has been seen since.

It seems probable to the writer that greater stability in standards of living will not be attained without a measure of decentralization of economic activity which will restore in a degree the best features of this earlier form of economic organization. I think there is some slight evidence of a tendency already in that direction, beneath the surface manifestations of increased concentration and centralization. But whether this is true or not, it is clear that the characteristics of modern business organization, including especially its centralization and concentration, have increased rather than diminished that tendency toward instability and inequality of distribution of prosperity which we have in mind when we discuss the problem of overproduction.

For, by overproduction we mean essentially instability of production from time to time and inequality of distribution of productive activity from place to place and as among products. We recognize that, so far at least, it cannot be said that more wealth is being produced in this world than its people want or can use. When we speak of overproduction we mean merely that in some places, at certain times, more of certain things is being produced than certain people want or can buy. Why this happens is the real problem.

As I see it the problem of overproduction is partly a matter of mechanics, and partly one of psychology. The mechanical problem relates to the technological methods of production and to the organization of production, distribution, and finance; the psychological problem enters also into the organization of production, distribution, and consumption. To put the matter another way, the problem of overproduction is a result of defects in the productive, distributive, financial, and consumptive aspects of our business organization, and these defects are partly mechanical and partly psychological. Governmental policies in matters of tariffs and immigration affect the distribution of goods and labor internationally and have a great deal to do with overproduction. But their effects are pervasive and fairly well recognized, and it is not necessary to say anything about them here. Aside from these, it seems to me that there are six main factors in the problem of overproduction: the use of power machinery; business organization; finance; the balance of production and consumption time; consumer psychology; and consumer purchasing power. The chief importance of tariffs, immigration restrictions, and other interferences with the mobility of products and labor is that, along with other factors, they give rise to what may be called geographical or local overproduction, which is merely a maldistribution of production from place to place. This aspect of overproduction seems to me less important, however, than that which results from the uneven distribution of productive activity in point of time and in point of types of product. It is in these respects that the factors just mentioned are most significant. They tend to break down the balance of what may be called the time equation of production, and the balance between the different types of productive activity. Although they are all important, limitation of space prevents me from saying very much about any of them except the factor of business organization.

In general, it seems to me that the tendency toward concentration and centralization in business organization has tended to create or at least intensify the problem of over-production. The main reasons for this conclusion may be stated briefly as follows:

1. The first phase of business concentration is an increase in the scale of production. This takes place in response to the desire to supply a larger market area than the older, small-scale, local industries could supply, as improved means of transportation and communication develop. It is facilitated by the use of more modern types of power and power-driven machinery, which have required the concentration of production in particular localities close to power sources, and made the operation of large units more economical. In the course of time, however, competition in these wider national markets has tended to increase and the costs of distribution have grown. The result has been increased emphasis upon low costs of production through increased volume of output. Although costs of production have thus been lowered as a result of concentration, these economies have been offset by increased costs of distribution in a wider market. Although wages in the concentrated industries have been increased as a result of economies in production, these increases have probably not offset the increased distributive costs in the whole market, so that the purchasing power of the entire market for the increased volume of production has probably not grown in proportion to the scale of production. Despite the fact that the most modern developments in the use of electric power permit a wider distribution of industrial activity in smaller units and thus a more even distribution of purchasing power and better access to local markets, these advantages have been almost wholly ignored, because of a belief in the superior profitableness of large-scale, concentrated production.

2. Such economies as have been achieved through industrial concentration have depended almost exclusively upon mass pro-

duction of standardized products. For a time, no doubt, this process has tended to widen the market by bringing the product within the range of purchasing power of a larger proportion of the population, and by increasing the purchasing power of those parts of the working population involved in the mass production industries. In the end, however, this process has tended to result in overproduction. It has involved constantly increasing volume of output per unit of time. This increase has not only led to increasing distribution costs, but it has tended to force up the rate of consumption per unit of time, which, beyond limits, tends to reduce values and prices. One reason for this breaking down of the time equation of production and consumption is that leisure for consumption has not increased as rapidly as the output during the working hours. Another equally important reason is that the increased purchasing power of those affected by the mass production industries has altered their consumption psychology. Instead of being satisfied with an increased consumption of standardized products within the time available, the consuming public has increasingly preferred to spend its larger purchasing power upon more individualized and varied products, especially in the United States where class or group standards of consumption are not fixed by custom or tradition. In short, the demand for increased leisure time for consumption and higher quality or greater individuality of products consumed has tended both to diminish, relatively, the amount of consumer purchasing power available for the low-priced, standardized mass products and to increase the average price level of goods and services most in consumer demand. The result has been an overproduction and undervaluation of standardized, mass products, and an underproduction or overvaluation of leisure, of services, and of products with individualistic quality appeal.

3. Overproduction due to industrial concentration has been fostered by mergers based on the false belief that the economies

of large-scale production and concentrated management insure greater profits to capital. In general it is probably true that industrial concentration through mergers has tended toward considerable purely technical economies in production. Such concentration has made it possible to eliminate obsolete machinery and install the most up-to-date production processes, as well as to improve production constantly through technological research. But these economies have, in most cases, been passed on to the immediate consumer in the form of lower prices and to workers in the form of higher wages, rather than to capital in the form of higher profits; and for the ultimate consumer they have been offset by higher distribution costs. Nor, so far as can be ascertained, has industrial concentration through mergers resulted in any measurable increase in stability of operations. For the most part, the tendency toward industrial concentration through mergers has not been the outcome of sound economic considerations. It has been fostered by banking and financial interests during periods of credit inflation and stock market booms, when money was readily available and securities could easily be sold to the public; and for the rest, it has been based upon the false belief that superior profits could be assured by control of the market. As a matter of fact, however, the profits of mergers, as well as their security prices, have shown in most cases no greater enhancement over a period of years than those of smaller independent concerns; and in very few cases, if any, has it been possible for such mergers to establish any real control of the market by control of production or maintenance of prices. The result has rather been increased volume of production, intensified competition, and lower market prices.

4. Overproduction would normally tend to cure itself by the process of natural economic selection through which the marginal or less efficient producer is eliminated. The prevailing tendencies in business organization, reflected not only in

mergers but in trade association activities, run counter to this process and thus tend to intensify the problem of overproduction. Mergers, being fostered largely from the point of view just described, result in most cases in protecting and maintaining the interests of the unsuccessful marginal independents which are absorbed. Although technically some excess capacity may be eliminated in the process of merger, the capital structure to be maintained by the volume of business is in most cases preserved or increased, and the whole tendency of the financial purposes behind mergers is to maintain the existing or increased capital structure by an increased volume of business. Where this is achieved for a time by restricting production so as to raise prices and increase profits through a dominant market position, the result is usually to lower the margin and bring new marginal producers into the field. The larger the merger and the more dominant its position in the market the more this tendency is emphasized. In fact, if the operations of the anti-trust laws were suspended entirely as regards mergers there is little reason to believe that the problem of overproduction would be in any way diminished. The same general principles apply to the efforts of trade organizations to control production or maintain prices in contravention of existing laws. The real tendency of these efforts is obviously to maintain all existing business interests in the field no matter how near the margin they may be. The more successful they are the greater the tendency to lower the margin and the more difficult the problem of production control. Here again if the existing laws restricting trade association activities were suspended the result would probably be not only the maintenance of all existing interests in the field but ultimately an increase in the number of producers, with a proportionate increase in the difficulties of production control.

These features of modern business organization, which can be only briefly summarized, seem to me to make it extremely unlikely that a solution of the problem of overproduction can be found in such increased concentration of business interests as is reflected in mergers and in the kind of trade association activities which are demanded by those who desire to see a revision of our anti-trust laws. In fact, the machine process of production is such that it inevitably tends to overproduction in proportion to the concentration of the interests which use it. The machine process itself is not a cause of overproduction and it does not necessarily imply concentration of business interests which use it. The only gain possible through concentration or cooperation of business interests using the machine process of production lies in the possibility of their better balancing the production of different types of goods and services; but such better balance has not been the result of the prevailing tendencies in business organization.

After all is said, the crux of the problem of overproduction lies in the field of consumption, and the main hope of its solution lies in the factors of finance, time, and consumer psychology.

Of these three factors the least promising of control is the last. Among the reasons for overproduction the least understood is that of changes in consumer psychology. This is more than a matter of alterations of taste, custom, or fashion in the demand for particular products. It does not seem to be realized that consumer demand, not only for particular things but for things in general, fluctuates from time to time and goes through cycles of greater or lesser intensity quite independently of changes in consumer purchasing power. These cycles are probably affected to some extent by the amount of leisure time available for consumption, but since such leisure is fairly stable or only slowly changing, it is likely that such cycles of buying desire would exist anyway. It is difficult to say how they arise, whether by occasional synchronism of phases of interest or ennui in masses of individuals, or as physiological phenomena; but there is evidence that they exist and play an important part in the so-called business cycle. It is possible that they may be an accompaniment of rapidly rising standards of living in which a multiplicity of goods and services are offered and available to consumers in rapidly increasing profusion; and that when the economic level of society has become more stabilized these cycles of buying interest or boredom may disappear. At any rate, the only means of mitigating them that suggests itself is through progressive increase of leisure time for consumption, which is indicated as necessary in any case to balance the time equation of production and consumption.

This balance of the time element in production and the time element in consumption, which I have referred to as the time equation in modern economic society, is only vaguely recognized as a factor in overproduction and its nature is very little understood. It is almost mathematically obvious, however, that there can be no close balance between production and consumption, in volume or value, unless there is a corresponding balance between the efficiency of production and what may be called the efficiency of consumption, both of which depend upon the capacity of output per unit of time, the capacity of consumption per unit of time, and the relative proportion of working and leisure time in society as a whole. As has been indicated, the result of mass production is greatly to increase the output per unit of time. This can be done mechanically, but unfortunately there are psychological obstacles in the way of proportionately increasing the time-rate of consumption. If more goods and services are offered to the consumer than he has time to utilize, their subjective value and ultimately the actual monetary value of these goods and services is bound to diminish. Time becomes proportionately more valuable to the consumer and goods proportionately cheaper to him under a process of mass consumption, just as labor time becomes more valuable and production cheaper to the employer under a process of mass production. One way of meeting the problem of overproduction, therefore, is to make power machinery yield a larger volume of output per unit of time, but to pay the worker for this larger output, not in terms of the product but in terms of the time saved. In short, working hours must be gradually shortened so as to provide increased consumer purchasing power in terms of leisure without reducing consumer purchasing power in terms of real wages or commodities and services.

If this is done, it is possible that some of the problems involved in consumer psychology, mentioned above, may find their solution. Cultural and non-material satisfactions have their economic value and can yield profits, employment, and wages to their producers, just as substantial commodities do. Increased purchasing power for such satisfactions, due to greater leisure, may help to turn the creative energies of society into new channels and effectively employ some of those energies now engaged in producing goods that are not wanted, even though there is money enough to buy them. In this way, payment in leisure may bring about a better balance as among types of products and activities, and so mitigate the problem of overproduction in certain industries.

After all, however, these factors in overproduction are significant only in relation to certain groups of the population. Fundamentally, for the great mass, underconsumption is not a question of time or of psychology but of actual purchasing power. It is here that the factor of our financial and banking organization and policies is of vital importance, and the possibilities of control are greatest. Although the balance in the time equation of production and consumption to which I have referred does not depend upon financial factors at all, there *is* a time lag between consumption and production in our modern business organization which is undoubtedly due to defects in our financial mechanism. It consists essentially in the fact that production is financed by credit or savings more rapidly or more often than consumption, which leads to the result that consumption periodically fails to keep pace with production because purchasing power does not flow back to consumers as rapidly as it flows into the channels of production.

In other words, in order to secure a better balance between production and consumption it is necessary somehow to supplement our system of production credit and of credit for primary distribution with a system of consumer credit through which purchasing power can be advanced to consumers somewhat ahead of productive activity. Installment selling is an effort in that direction, but it is defective in certain respects, which I have not space to discuss here. What is needed is not a special extension of credit of a particular kind for the purchase of particular products by consumers, but a control of the general expansion and contraction of bank credit in relation to changes in the volume of production and trade. If the amount of purchasing medium in circulation, today almost wholly a credit medium, can be closely controlled in keeping with changes in the rate of growth of industry and trade, conditions of overproduction and underconsumption, with their reflection in declining prices, may be avoided.

The responsibility for this general control rests primarily on our banking system and financial institutions. So far as general credit control is concerned, there has undoubtedly been considerable progress in recent years. Although the technique is far from perfected, the general principles are fairly well understood and the machinery for applying them —which must be international in scope—is being developed. But in concrete and specific practical issues, banks and investment institutions have to bear a great deal of the blame for conditions of overproduction in specific industries and at certain times. In the financing of specific enterprises and especially of mergers and consolidations, financial institutions appear to be working mostly in the dark, without regard to the conditions of industrial capacity, supply and demand in particular lines, which should be carefully studied before financing is undertaken. If we had a supreme dictator or economic planning council which could undertake to allocate new capital through lines of industrial development in the light of market conditions and social needs it might be a much simpler problem to prevent overdevelopment and excess production than it is where these matters are left to private initiative and individual judgment. It would appear, however, that there is opportunity for greater cooperation among banks and financial institutions toward better control in this respect even under a system of private initiative. Until such cooperation and control are developed it is likely that a condition of unbalanced production as between types of products and different localities will persist. The resulting strain and stress, however, can be borne and is not likely to lead to general instability, if the broader type of general credit control through our central banking system is fully and effectively exercised.

XVII

MANAGEMENT AND OVERPRODUCTION

By H. S. PERSON

Managing Director of Taylor Society, New York

ECONOMISTS have consistently considered *production* as comprehending that total cycle of operations which includes the procurement of crude materials, their conversion into consumable form, and their physical distribution to ultimate consumers; and have employed the word *distribution* to identify the concept of distribution of the resultant social income in the form of profits, rent, interest, salaries, and wages. Business men, on the other hand, have used the word *production* to identify the fabrication process, and the word *distribution* to identify the physical distribution of the resultant goods. The business man's distinction has been based on the fact that in the organization of industry there has been a division of labor among enterprises with respect to the operations involved, some devoting themselves to fabrication and some to physical distribution. The economist's refusal to make a distinction has been based on the fact that all these processes are fundamentally identical in that they represent only differences in methods of the creation of utilities—form, place, quantity, time, etc.—demanded by consumers. They assert correctly that the same basic problems of management are involved in the creation of all utilities, whether they be form, time, or place utilities. There is promise that experience with recent developments such as hand-to-mouth buying and selling direct to consumer will bring to business realization that the same principles of management govern both fabrication and physical distribution, and will bring business to the economist's point of view; in which case one step will have been taken toward unification and clarification of thinking about such problems as overproduction.

With respect to the concept of *overproduction,* the economist has been too narrow in his views. Taking the long run point of view he has declared that goods are ultimately bought with goods and that production and consumption must eventually balance. Although he has been compelled to recognize what he calls an occasional temporary excess of goods relative to the effective demand for those goods, he dismisses that aspect of the matter by asserting that price changes will effect a new balance and clings to his generalization that in the long run there can be no overproduction. On the other hand, the business man is acutely conscious that a temporary excess of goods relative to effective demand is a real and not infrequent experience, and that related to it are unemployment, disappearance of profits, sometimes bankruptcy, and other serious social problems. In these days of division of labor, specialization, and credit economy, such maladjustments, even if only temporary, are very far-reaching, and the business man knows, the economist to the contrary notwithstanding, that there is such a thing as overproduction. A second step toward clearer thinking and wiser action will have been taken were the economist to recognize the weight of the business man's view of overproduction.

Common recognition that the business man's production and distribution are only superficially different and are representative of the same principles of management, and common recognition that there is such a thing as overproduction, will promote a common attack by business men and economists on the problem of overproduction, and especially will promote recognition of the fact that some measure of solution of the problem may result from better managements by owners of their individual enterprises and better management by industrial society of its inter-related and integrated industries.

In the field of management of industrial enterprises Frederick W. Taylor was the creative genius with respect to managerial practice and the analysis of this practice. He gave industry a body of principles which constitute the science governing effective management.[1] Without discussion of the nature and origin of scientific management let us turn immediately to the most recent statement of its principles:[2]

1. *Management Research.* Research, investigation, and experiment (with their processes of analysis, measurement, comparison, etc.) constitute the only sound basis for the solution of managerial problems; for determinations of purpose, policy, program, project, product, material, machine, tool, type of ability or skill, method, and other factors, and the coordination of these in purposeful effort.

2. *Management Standards.* To make them useful to an enterprise, the results of research, investigation, and experiment must be made available to the cooperating group in the form of defined and published standards which serve as common goals, facilities, and methods, and which replace chance and variable factors by constants in terms of which may be made calculations and plans which may be expected to come true.

3. *Management Control.* There must be established a systematic procedure, based on the defined standards, for the execution of work; a procedure which directs the researches, establishes and maintains the standards, initiates operations, and controls work in process; which facilitates each specialized effort and coordinates all specialized efforts, to the end that the common objectives may be achieved with a minimum of waste

---

[1] Cf. "Frederick W. Taylor, Father of Scientific Management," by Frank Barkley Copley, New York, Harper & Brothers, 1923, 2 Vols.

[2] "Scientific Management in American Industry," by the Taylor Society (H. S. Person, Editor), New York, Harper & Brothers, 1929.

of human and material energies, and with a maximum of human welfare and contentment.

4. *Cooperation.* Durably effective management requires recognition of the natural laws of cooperation; involves the integration of individual interests and desires with group interests and desires and of individual capacities with the requirements of group purposes; the substitution of the laws of situations for individual authority, guess, and whim; and the recognition and capitalization of human differences, motives, desires, and capacities in the promotion of a common purpose.

If the reader will for a while ponder over this statement of principles and explore their implications, he will perceive that they have a direct bearing on the menace of overproduction. They establish in the place of management which is highly opportunistic, speculative, and unregulated, that which is predetermined and controlled. They involve measurement of industrial conditions and tendencies and of the state of market demands, and a program of production in the inclusive sense of the word through control of the facilities by which the demands may be satisfied; and they imply increase of the probability that those demands will be satisfied with a minimum of waste. If all industrial concerns were managed in accordance with these principles, there would be reduction of maladjusted production, unemployment, and other related phenomena to a degree that would be astounding.

These principles are already extensively expressed in the art of managing throughout industry, but only in a few instances are *all* of them expressed in any one particular management. The spread of their influence has been rather a result of casual imitation of elements of the art which expresses them than the result of planned efforts of a creative leadership which takes all principles and their complete application into consideration. Therefore, an excellent expression of one or two principles, but not of others, may be found in one enterprise, and a different combination in another enterprise. But the problem of over-production, insofar as it can be eliminated by the aggregate of managements of individual enterprises, will be eliminated only to the degree that all enterprises express all of the principles in all phases of the art of managing.

An enterprise managed in accordance with these principles will exhibit the following items of conduct in its art of managing:

1. A policy of development over a considerable period will be formulated. This policy will represent not merely desires and ambitions but reasonable expectations based on investigations of industrial and market conditions and tendencies generally, and with respect to the commodity items with which the particular enterprise is concerned. It will be represented in a schedule of growth which is fairly even and will avoid over-extension in times of boom and serious retrenchment in times of depression. It will look upon boom periods as offering temptations which must be resisted, and dull times as imposing obstacles which must be overcome. It will include a schedule of balanced investments in plant, equipment, and labor skills which will precisely care for the predetermined growth of the enterprise.

2. This enterprise will provide for a function, which we shall identify as merchandising, which lies between development policy on the one hand and the execution of production (including sales) plans on the other hand. A retail merchant is rated by his competitors as a good merchandiser when he "buys the right goods in the right quantities at the right times" and keeps them moving in ceaseless flow on to his consumers. Likewise, a manufacturer is a good merchandiser when he fabricates the right commodities of the right materials in the right quantities at the right times and keeps them moving in a ceaseless flow through his outlets. This merchandising is different from and something larger than selling; it consists of planning

for both fabrication and selling as parts of an integral and continuous whole of effort. It establishes in master budgets and schedules the task of the entire organization, and in detail budgets and schedules of fabrication, sales, finance, and employment, the separate but complementary tasks of the various operating departments.

3. The purchase of materials and their fabrication will proceed in accordance with 'he schedules which are derived from the master merchandising schedule, and at costs which have been predetermined. This is rendered practicable by a precise control of all the factors which enter into the processes involved—machines, tools, methods, skills, and a regulated flow of materials into processes, all in accordance with the best which experience and experiment have made available.

4. Selling will be planned and conducted in a similar manner in accordance with the master merchandising schedule. Quotas by commodities, territories, and salesmen will be established and each quota will be a definite goal for achievement. Sales pressure will be intensified when times are dull and resistance greatest, through additional special salesmen, increased advertising, and release of new and novel items. It may be relaxed, and the released energies applied elsewhere, when selling is easy. Always the dominant interest should be conformity to development policy and accomplishment of the master merchandising schedules.

5. In accordance with the master merchandising schedule and the complementary fabrication and selling schedules, will be constructed a financial schedule which will guide the treasurer or comptroller in arranging for the availability of working capital. He will have standards by which to control loans and repayments at the bank, loans in the form of bills and accounts payable, investment in equipment, inventories and receivables; and in general he will keep fixed capital at a minimum and working capital liquid.

6. Similarly, employment and training of the working force will be in accordance with a schedule which reflects all other operating schedules and the general development policy. The payroll will be reduced to the limit of adequacy, yet increased in accordance with development plans, and will be made up of the precisely necessary quantities of essential skills. Good will will be developed by steadiness of employment and wage policy, and the inherent efficiency of research-discovered best methods will be brought out by labor's good will and interest in every phase of operating.

If all industrial enterprises were inspired to develop their arts of management along the lines which have been described, overproduction would be so reduced as practically to disappear as a serious problem. But we must frankly admit that it does not appear likely that, if left to individual initiative influenced solely by exhortation, the improvement of management generally will be sufficiently rapid to constitute a remedy for unemployment. The habits fixed by individualistic frontier industry, when demand generally was always ahead of supply, are still too strong. It may require some great general emotional reaction to some greater crisis in our industrial life than we have yet experienced, to generate a general impulse toward an art of managing which will take advantage of what we have already learned about the science of management.

Europe has been through such a crisis and as a consequence is responding to an urge for wide application of the principles of scientific management. This urge is not only for generally better management of individual enterprises, but for better management by society of its industries. *Rationalization* would apply the principles of scientific management to entire industries and to all the industries of a country. What in our American experience the coordination of well-managed departments of an individual plant has been to scientific management of individual plants, the coordination of well-managed plants in an entire industry, and of well-managed industries in an entire country, mean to rationalization.

Rationalization appears to have had its origin in Germany. Just as Frederick W. Taylor is recognized by Europe as the father of scientific management, so Walter Rathenau may be recognized by us as the father of rationalization. Taylor originated the concept of an inclusive technique of management for the individual plant; Rathenau formulated the concept of more efficient organization and management of entire industries. Taylor's genius was in the origination of a technique; Rathenau's in the concept of a social organization of industry in terms of modern technique. Rathenau, it should be borne in mind, was no theoretical utopian; he was director in some eighty-six German and twenty-one foreign enterprises, representing a score of different industries, an organizer of cartels, managing director of A. E. G., the great electrical combine of Germany, and the organizer of the industrial resources of Germany during the war. He was the author of several books expounding his ideas, of which the most noteworthy appeared just before and during the war.[3] These books at first did not make an impression on those in control of European industry.

The war prepared the soil of European industry for germination of the seeds of thought which had been sowed by Rathenau. War weary, their industries apparently destroyed, Germany and all Europe immediately after the war turned to whatever promised speedy and effective reorganization of an industrial society disorganized by the war. There was the doctrine of social organization of industry which had been advanced by Rathenau; there was the technique of scientific management which had been developed in the United States. What more promising than application of the principles of sci-

---

[3] "Criticism of the Age" (1912), "In Days to Come" (1917), "The New Economy" (1918), "The New State" (1919), and "The New Society" (1919).

entific management on the scale suggested by Rathenau? To this new ideal was attached the name rationalization, and the concept has come to pervade all of European industry.

The following definition of rationalization by an impartial English student is a fair one, if the words combination and amalgamation are taken in their generic rather than in too narrow a technical or legal sense; but it should be realized that every country of Europe has its own definition which reflects its philosophic and legal attitude toward social institutions:[4]

Rationalization is the process of associating together individual undertakings or groups of firms in a close form of amalgamation, and ultimately of unifying, in some practicable degree of combination, whole industries, both nationally and internationally; with the allied objects (beyond what is possible to an industry divided into many competitive units) of increasing efficiency, lowering costs, improving conditions of labour, promoting industrial co-operation, and reducing the waste of competition, these objects being achieved by various means which unification alone makes in full measure available—the regulation of the production of an industry to balance the consumption of its products; the control of prices; the logical allocation of work to individual factories; the stabilization of employment and regularization of wages; the standardization of materials, methods and products; the simplification of the ranges of goods produced; the economical organization of distribution; the adoption of scientific methods and knowledge in the management and technique of trades as a whole; and the planning and pursuit of common trade policies.

Or, to use the terms already employed in this discussion, rationalization is that form of industrial combination which is undertaken with the object of widening the scope for the application of scientific management to the extent of whole industries, and achieving the benefits to producers, consumers, and the community which scientific management conducted on this scale alone can provide.

---

[4] Oliver Sheldon in "What is Rationalisation?" in *Industrial Welfare* (London), March, 1929, p. 85.

In a word, rationalization is not combination, nor is it scientific management; it is, rather, a form of the one with the object of the fullest extension of the other.

A great variety of experiments along the line of rationalization are being undertaken in Europe. At the one extreme are the efforts of the dictatorships of Russia and of Italy; at the other extreme the hesitating steps of individualistic England. Germany may be placed perhaps midway between the two. Through all these experiments there runs a unity of purpose— reorganization and strengthening of industry through state influence either in the form of direct control or less formally organized leadership. The degree to which scientific management is employed varies directly with the degree of understanding of that technique, which in practice is moderate even where intellectual acceptance is pronounced.

That the doctrine of rationalization will have influence in the United States just as the doctrine of scientific management has influence in Europe is probable. Its principal objective is regularization of industry on a large scale; and present experience with the paradox of huge production and unemployment in the United States, the present concern over a "menace of overproduction," promises to direct American attention to the European doctrine. Some slight unconscious steps toward rationalization have already been taken: The organization of the Bureau of Simplified Commercial Practice in the Department of Commerce, the organization and work under Hoover influence of the Committee on Elimination of Waste in Industry, and the President's Conference on Unemployment; the appointment of the United States Coal Commission; the National Business Survey Conference following the stock market debacle in November of last year; the Wagner unemployment bills;— these indicate an increasing compulsion of circumstances toward taking thought about and doing something about industrial regularization on a national scale. But there has been as yet no situation in the United States sufficiently critical to generate the emotional impulse for a positive step in the direction of rationalization. It is more likely to be generated eventually by the problems arising out of the developments of the control of power and radio communication under the direction of an as yet highly individualistic industrial society.

The principal objective of rationalization is regularized increase of national industrial power. The principal objective of scientific management has been regularized increase of the industrial power of the individual plant. In principle the concepts are identical; in practice the techniques must be identical. The principal difference is the plane or area of application. To the popular mind the appeal of scientific management has been its power to increase productivity. To the mind of the plant in which scientific management has become established, its appeal is its power of control of the situation—control up or control down in productivity, according to requirements of established policy and the immediate situation:

But I can bear witness tonight, from actual experience, that without scientific management we should not have been able so securely to meet the decline in prices and in business which we have had to meet during the past year; that without the greater knowledge and greater control which scientific management has given, we should not have been able, in the concerns in which I am interested, to get production down to match demand . . . and still make both ends meet. . . . It has interested me to observe the greater precision with which scientific management has enabled us to meet the situation. . . .[5]

Scientific Management is not merely a national weapon to increase production; it is a national weapon to control production. It controls increase; it controls decrease; and in either instance it can control with stabilization. This has been dem-

---

[5] Henry P. Kendall in *Bulletin of the Taylor Society*, Vol. VII, No. 2, April, 1922.

onstrated in individual plants, and in groups of plants under individual ownership and centralized management policy harmonized with decentralized operating authority. It can be utilized for the control of the industries of a nation, either through the voluntary and independent development of scientific management in all enterprises or through its development in all enterprises under a form of suasion suggested by the concept of rationalization.

XVIII

MORE EVIDENCE AND A SUMMARY

OVERPRODUCTION IN AGRICULTURE AND FORESTS

SOMETHING is radically wrong with our largest industry—agriculture. Dr. Baker goes straight to the cause. The farmers continue to produce more than they can sell at a profit. The use of marginal land for crops, instead of for timber growing and pastures, discourages the use of fertilizers. The failure to use more fertilizer encourages in turn the use of marginal land. A new national land policy is essential.

A careful survey of nearly 300,000,000 acres of land in the north-central and southeastern United States has shown, says Dr. Lipman, that 40 per cent of it is marginal. In his opinion the farm relief problem is world-wide. When we relieve the good agricultural land from the unfair and destructive competition of marginal acres, we shall point the way to a more prosperous agriculture. Our 300,000,000 acres of arable land undergo a net loss of 3,000,000 to 4,000,000 tons of nitrogen annually.

The rate of depletion of our timber resources discourages the farmer from planting his marginal land to trees. It determines in large measure the price. The market value of pulp wood and lumber is for the most part the actual labor cost of cutting and transportation. The cost of timber growing, fire protection, etc., does not enter into the price.

When the waste of fire and excessive cutting are both taken into account, it appears that the rate of depletion is four times the rate of growth for the entire country. Only two-fifths of the original stand remains.

OVERPRODUCTION IN COAL

The real problem of the bituminous mining industry arises from the existence of excess capacity. The industry, explains Mr. Bockus, has acquired the habit of expanding to meet the constantly increasing demand. During the last decade there has been no increase in the demand. The average annual output for the three years 1917–1918–1919 amounted to 532,000,000 net tons, while during the years 1927–1928–1929 it was only 517,000,000 tons.

The unrestrained effort of individual operators to utilize their own capacity when conditions in the market made it certain that large amounts of capacity must go unutilized has driven the price of bituminous coal to its present unprofitable level. Low prices impose a limit upon the percentage of coal recovered in mine operations.

The British Industrial Transference Board reported in 1928 on the excess capacity in the coal industry of Great Britain. The Board found that there were at least 200,000 miners permanently out of a job, and that a similar situation existed in other industries.

OVERPRODUCTION IN OIL

Competition has been carried too far. In the opinion of Sir Henri Deterding it is forcing the production of oil in excess of the world's needs. The big companies are compelled to create duplication of facilities and a corresponding waste of human energy and capital. The consuming and producing areas of the world are thrown out of balance. There is no way of balancing the rate of exhaustion of the principal sources of supply. Conservation, in the oil industry at least, is the only way to eliminate the evils of overproduction, the only sensible way to bring order out of chaos.

As in the case of so many other industries, the oil industry in this country is suffering from the overexpansion that took place during the war period. Petroleum production was greatly increased, explains Mr. Salisbury, to meet war requirements.

Today the industry with a world market for 4,000,000 barrels daily is carrying an overhead based upon actual shut-in production of 5,950,000 barrels per day—more than 48 per cent above its existing requirements.

With daily oil production nearly always exceeding consumption, above-ground storage has been continuously increasing, and during the last seven years there has been accumulated above ground in the United States alone, about 305,000,000 barrels of crude and products.

This overproduction is far-reaching in its effect. The overproduction of crude involves the overproduction of fuel oil. The overproduction of fuel oil involves the coal and oil industries in wasteful competition. And waste in production involves waste in distribution.

OVERPRODUCTION IN THE TEXTILES

The war-time demand for cotton goods, says Mr. Kendall, was so great that every mill could sell its output at a profit, and production was accelerated tremendously, especially in the South where labor laws permitted night operation. The long hours of work in cotton textiles have been one of the main roots of overproduction.

Depressions in the cotton textile industry have recurred with such insistence that they may be said to have become chronic. On

day and night runs the industry has a productive capacity of some-
where between 135 and 140 per cent of consumption.

It is futile to debate whether the troubles of the industry are
due to overproduction or underconsumption, as long as goods are
produced in such quantities that they cannot be absorbed into the
stream of demand at prices permitting of a fair profit.

The potential capacity of the wool industry, says Mr. A. D.
Whiteside, exceeds current demand by a wide margin.   In
1927 the consumption of woolen and worsted fabrics amounted
to approximately $656,000,000, as compared with a maximum
manufacturing capacity of $1,750,000,000 at current prices.

Potential production figures for the weaving and spinning divisions of the woolen and worsted piece goods and yarn divisions
of the wool industry, furnish a rough measure of excess capacity.

1929

Weaving Division

Potential Production	Actual Consumption	%
$1,465,000,000	$550,000,000	37.5

Spinning Division

Potential Production	Actual Consumption	%
232,000,000 pounds	83,109,139 pounds	35.8

Wool Machinery Activity

COMBS

Per cent of activity to total—Average for twelve months

1924	1928
73.7	66.4

United States Department of Commerce

In the years during and immediately after the World War,
says Mr. Hill, mills were started in hundreds of small villages,

throughout the state of Pennsylvania particularly, and through the New England states. It was during these years that silk manufacturers found themselves in the same position as many other groups that were bending all their energies to meeting demand by improved methods and machinery, increased plants, multiple shifts, and all the other factors utilized in speeding up production of this type of merchandise.

The industry must find an answer to the problem of adjustment of mass production to a product controlled by style.

OVERPRODUCTION IN THE AUTOMOTIVE INDUSTRY

The automotive industry of the United States maintains a reserve capacity that is far in excess of normal requirements. Notwithstanding this potential capacity, plant is still increased and production schedules are boosted in the belief that sales will keep pace with the increase in volume.

In the plans of the Ford Company for production of facilities in 1930 more than $20,000,000 was to be spent for new buildings and additions to plant, and more than $10,000,000 for equipment. Packard's plans called for the addition of 375,000 square feet of floor space; Hudson, 40,000 square feet; Oldsmobile, 35,000 square feet, etc.

The potential output of the automotive industry is probably inflated in proportions not far different from those of many of our other industries, such as coal, oil, agriculture, etc. It is the excess of potential capacity in all our basic industries which constitutes the depressing factor in modern business.

Automobile manufacturers are well enough informed regarding the volume of sales, but lack information as to the rate of expansion of their competitors, or the rate of expansion of other industries.

While the largest actual monthly output multiplied by

twelve gives our only index to the theoretical possible output, actual output would have to be somewhat smaller. In the automobile industry changes in models necessarily slow down production. Continuous operation would call for larger storage facilities.

Based on the output for April of last year, the automotive industry had a theoretical capacity of 8,000,000 units. This is nearly twice as many as have ever been produced or sold in a year. Competition, under these conditions, fails to encourage a distribution of the increasing demand between existing plants.

It may very well be that in the course of time the automotive industry in this country will grow up to its present probable capacity of 8,000,000 units per year; it may exceed that number. But we cannot afford to disregard the simple fact that the production of motor vehicles in the United States, Canada, and Europe in 1929 totalled only 6,295,352. The United States alone had the capacity to supply more than the world's requirements.

Factories in the United States and Canada were responsible for more than 89 per cent of the world's total production of motor vehicles in 1929, as compared with 88 per cent in 1928. To conclude that this percentage will continue to increase, or even be maintained, is to discourage the growth of manufacturing abroad.

In the last analysis the automotive industry is only entitled to a proportion of the total income spent for food, clothing, etc. To anticipate more than its rightful share of income is sure to induce wasteful competition between industries and nations.

OVERPRODUCTION IN OTHER INDUSTRIES

The Federated American Engineers Society in its study of "Waste in Industry" found idle capacity in many of our industries. The committee was agreed that productive capacity should be conservatively based upon careful study of normal demand. Uniform production was advised as a way of coping with and satisfying nation-wide variation in demand. This could be attained through storing in slack times and releasing in boom times.

The potential capacity of our shoe plants was very large. With a capacity of 1,750,000 pairs of shoes per day, the average production was about 977,000 pairs for a 300-day year. The overequipment in the printing industry amounted to over 50 per cent. This represented hundreds of millions of dollars of idle equipment, to say nothing of other overhead charges. The Committee found that 750,000 workers in the coal-mining industry were idle during a substantial portion of the year.

The steel industry of the United States has a rated capacity of 62,265,270 tons of ingots per year. Last year showed a record output of 56,433,473 tons. The United States Steel expansion program for this year comprised more than one-half of that of the entire industry. An average expansion of 1,200,000 tons has been realized by the entire industry for the past thirty years. This year's expansion program called for 4,000,000 tons.

Mr. Leonard Kuvin estimates that the steel industry operates at 60 to 80 per cent of its possible capacity. In the February issue of the Taylor Society Bulletin, he draws attention to a number of estimates of idle capacity in other industries. Mr. E. F. Du Brul estimates that the machine tool industry has operated for the past ten years at an average of 65 per cent. Dr. Joseph E. Pogue conservatively estimates that the oil refineries of the country operate about 76 per cent of their rated productive capacity. Mr. H. E. Bates estimates that the manufacturing gas industry operates at 66 per cent of its total productivity. In a recent report of the Federal

Trade Commission, Edmund Brown, Jr., estimates the total productive capacity of the nations' flour mills at two and a half times their greatest production.

In the study of performance standards the American Engineers' Society found a wide difference between the standards in the best and average plants. There were boot and shoe factories where the output was two pairs per man per day, and others where it was twelve pairs. There were blast furnaces where it took one man an hour and twelve minutes to produce a ton of iron, and other blast furnaces where it took one man eleven hours to produce a ton. There were sawmills where the output was 15 board-feet per man hour, and others where it was 323 board-feet.

The Federal Bureau of Labor statistics are quoted by James O'Connell and John P. Frey, for the statement that if all blast furnaces were as efficient as the most efficient the present production of pig iron could be attained by the work of 3,000 men instead of 28,000; similarly, 45,000 men could then do the work now being done by 292,000 men in sawmills; 420,000 miners could do the work now requiring 750,000, and 80 per cent of all brickmakers now employed would be out of a job if the brickmaking machine producing 49,000 bricks per hour with one worker became universal, while if all boot and shoe factories operated as efficiently as the best equipped, 28,084 workers would turn out the same amount now done by 196,585 workers.

Some authorities in this country estimate that our machines are idle over 30 per cent of the time. Mr. Wallace Clark estimates that the plants in which he has been engaged at various times operate at 40 to 60 per cent of their productive capacity.

WHAT IS OVERPRODUCTION?

Perhaps the thing that is most baffling about overproduction is the definition of the term itself.

The average business man limits its application to what

might be called *actual* overproduction, *i.e.,* production of more of a commodity than consumers want or can buy. A far more significant definition lies in more plant, more capital investment than can be efficiently utilized.

Before the 19th century, the tendency to produce beyond market requirements was non-existent or at most local in character. The real problem of industry was to produce in sufficient quantity to supply the demand. At a later date the tendency to produce beyond market requirements became general and permanent.

Back of the business fluctuations of today is a potential capacity; a capacity to produce consistently more goods than income can absorb. The cost of maintaining this idle capacity has brought into general operation the law of diminishing income returns; the law which says that modern productive capacity cannot increase out of proportion to buying capacity, without further destroying consuming power.

In other words, potential producing and consuming capacity must be balanced, if the peaks and valleys of capital-labor employment are to be leveled out; if production is to be rationalized and drastic recessions eliminated.

Overproduction or excess capacity eludes exact measurement because we have no accurate measuring rod. Profits, wealth, and income are factors of the first importance in measuring the rate of industrial expansion; and they are hopelessly confused.

PROFITS, WEALTH, AND INCOME HOPELESSLY CONFUSED

Before the advent of power machinery, man's capacity to produce a surplus, over and above his immediate needs, was small. Mankind for the most part was forced to accept as inevitable the drudgery of unremitting toil.

The United States Department of Agriculture by actual

experimenting with spades has found that a laborer with a spade cannot within the time limits of the planting season, prepare more than a certain small area of ground for planting, and that area is barely sufficient to raise food for his own sustenance. The American farmer of seventy-five years ago had his hands full in taking care of twelve crop acres. Today he can handle thirty-four.

The early 19th century saw power machinery, steam navigation, and railway transportation coming into use. They facilitated a division of labor and the separation of industries. The power was thus acquired to produce a general surplus for exchange.

This surplus transformed "money-making" and "money-spending" into a common practice. It stimulated the growth of commerce and manufacturing to such an extent that they emerged during the 19th century to take a ranking position with agriculture as basic world industries.

The production of a general surplus was a leaven in more ways than one. Better food, better hygiene, and fewer famines all contributed to extend the life span and increase man's efficiency. The same causes contributed to an increase in the birth-rate and a decrease in the death-rate. As a result the human race reached a rate of increase during the 19th century that was enormously great as compared with anything known to the past. A world population of approximately 640,000,000 in 1800 now numbers close to 2,000,000,000 human beings.

These increasing numbers stimulated for the time being the activity of industry and the production of wealth. The wealth of Great Britain, France, and the United States, which was approximately 8, 7, and 1 billion dollars respectively in 1800, had increased to 121, 58, and 349 billion dollars by 1928.

Steam power according to Mulhall constituted in 1840 5 per cent of the working power of Christendom. By 1895 it was equal to the aggregate force of men and horses of all nations. The 39,000,000 horsepower employed in the factories of the United States in 1927 did the equal of work performed by 390,000,000 workers. The total prime moving capacity in this country today is close to 800,000,000 horsepower. This is about four times as great as that of Great Britain or Germany, and ten times as great as that of France.

As the power to produce a surplus became general, the need developed for making a clearer distinction between gross and net profits; between profits and income.

The rapid growth of the corporate form of business during the last century gave rise to a multitude of stockholders, wage earners and managers. Profits had to be divided in such a way as to satisfy the stockholders, pay wages and salaries, and keep the capital investment intact. The closer valuation of these several factors in production contributed to a clarification of terms.

This clarification continued during the first half of the 19th century. The ordinary running expense, such as wages, salaries, interest, taxes were included in the cost of upkeep. Depreciation and obsolescence were added to the list. The policy was developed of plowing back into business a fair proportion of the income.

The latter half of the century was marked by growing confusion. Larger profits and keener competition encouraged property owners to defer some of the fixed charges. The costs of depreciation and obsolescence were often neglected. Reserve funds were employed to an increasing extent in the expansion of plant facilities. Out of the increase in volume, industry anticipated a return sufficiently large to meet all deficiencies.

But industry was not counting the growing cost of maintaining a reserve of man power and machines. Interest and dividends paid on idle capacity began to encroach on the surplus intended eventually for the upkeep account. Good intentions were further sidetracked by the seemingly growing advantages that attached to excess capacity. It could be used to take up the slack in modern business. It could be used to force consolidations, control production and prices. It could be used to secure orders when demand was at the peak. It could be used to kill off competitors and hold markets in anticipation of better times.

In order to cover up the losses due to excess capacity, industry appropriated natural resources on an ever-increasing scale, and transferred this capital as profits into the income account. Notwithstanding rising costs of production and decreasing returns, Great Britain increased her output of coal 62,000,000 tons annually during the first thirteen years of the 20th century. This rate of expansion did not account for the increase in productivity of other countries. Profits that belonged in the up-keep account went into expansion.

By capitalizing an artificial increase in income wrung from natural resources and covering it with issues of securities bearing fixed charges, industry has attained a rate of expansion which is all out of proportion to the actual growth of income.

In thus appropriating capital for the income account, we have all but destroyed the line of demarcation between wealth, profits, and income. This transfer of capital gave rise to the belief that capital could be converted into income and income into capital.

Income can be converted into capital, but the conversion can only be accomplished through investment. The purchase of food or clothing does not constitute such an investment. Neither is the rise in the value of securities real income. It is quite true that we term this rise, book income. At the same time we term the depreciation of these securities a capital loss. This lax use of terms has facilitated the transfer of capital into the income account. The appropriation of natural resources on an ever-increasing scale eludes measurement.

This confusion regarding terms has made many people conclude that there was no such thing as capital dissipation; that there was no hard and fast line to be drawn between national income and national capital; that in a broad sense capital and income were not separate things but different ways of measuring the same thing.

Capital, under modern conditions, is a reservoir only as long as the cost of upkeep of the capital-labor investment is met from year to year. Income is a flow only as long as the cost of capital-labor upkeep is met from year to year. By capital-labor upkeep we mean the bare cost of maintaining the investment or "going concern" intact. It constitutes a fixed overhead on a standard investment of labor and capital. This overhead is covered by a minimum wage paid to the capital and labor investors on a standard of performance. The standard of capital-labor performance is sufficiently high to cover the cost of depreciation, replacement, obsolescence, interest on bonds, rent, taxes, insurance, and the minimum wage paid to the labor investors. Earnings over and above the cost of upkeep constitute income.

To disregard the cost of upkeep is to foster a rate of industrial expansion that is out of proportion to the slower growth of income. By neglecting to employ the time factor in the measurement of capital we have unwittingly allowed the capital reservoir to fill with silt.

The flow of income is comparable in many respects to the flow of a river. When the forest covering which tends to stabilize the flow of the river is removed, the flow is no longer subject to regulation; it becomes torrential. Under these conditions silt is carried down in increasing quantities into the reservoir.

Income today is a torrential stream. Reserve capacity is like the silt that collects from deforested land.

Profits cannot be depended upon any longer to supply the

wherewithal to pay for food, clothing, insurance, radios, education, vacations, etc. Higher standards of living cannot continue to be financed out of a speculative increase in capital values, out of the profits derived from boom periods of expansion. The profit incentive today places a premium on expansion, a premium on peak demand. But *income* rightly understood, places a premium on continued prosperity, on normal demand.

No nation is realizing an income return on its capital-labor investment. Close to half the corporations of the United States are operating at a deficit, and the proportion is steadily increasing. The total gross income for companies with no net profits amounted in 1925 to over 24 billion dollars. The net return of all corporations in 1922 was about 5¾ per cent.

ACCELERATION IN CONSUMPTION

The desire for what the economist calls "higher standards of living" is common today to all classes and nations. It is a universal objective. In India the man who is suffering from hunger wants more food. In the United States, where most people have enough to eat and enough to wear, the man who has no automobile wants one; the man who has an automobile wants two; the man who has two wants a motor boat; and so on *ad lib*.

But higher standards of living make greater demands upon the soil, timber, mineral, and water resources. The diversified diet of modern man exacts a much larger toll from the soil. Modern industry has multiplied its demands upon the soil as well as upon the mineral and water resources. Farms furnish 30 to 40 per cent of the raw materials upon which the modern factory works.

Into the service of the new industrial, commercial and agricultural society, have been drawn minerals and soil resources at an unprecedented rate. Resources such as coal, iron, copper, lead, oil, phosphates, potash, etc., which lay almost untouched during the ages, were transformed into necessities essential to the realization and preservation of "higher standards of living."

The British Empire and the United States together produce over two-thirds of the 2 billion tons of mineral products that the world consumes annually. The world has used more of its mineral resources in the last twenty years, according to C. K. Leith, than in all preceding history.

The fact that the mineral resources of the world are limited in amount and irregularly distributed, has transformed the character of international trade. Today there is an organic relationship between the nations. The flow of international trade must be rationalized, if the related development of the nations is to be assured.

We have consistently refused to take into account the increasing draft upon natural resources that attended a rise in living standards. With 2 billion people in all nations seeking to realize "higher standards of living," there is no escaping this levy.

With no nation meeting the cost of upkeep of its capital-labor investment in advance of expansion; with one billion people still living close to a bare subsistence level; with more and more of the earnings that belong in the upkeep account going into expansion, it is impossible to say what the cost of upkeep would be of 2 billion people living above a subsistence level. Neither have we any clear idea as to the increased draft upon the natural resources required to meet this cost of upkeep.

As a matter of fact we do not know whether the natural resources of the world could continue to support, for any length of time, 2 billion people living above a subsistence level. We can gain this knowledge, however, by bringing our rate of industrial expansion under control. Conservation, it is now only too clear, is no longer a question of altruism. It is an absolute necessity.

FORCES MAKING FOR EXPANSION

The tariff, the income tax, profits, corporations, etc., are forces which formerly served as brakes and governor upon the rate of industrial expansion. The machinery of expansion was in low gear. We have with us today a high-power machinery of production that is being operated without the brakes and governor of an earlier period. This release encourages every industry and nation to expand to the limit.

TARIFF NO LONGER BRAKE ON EXPANSION

There were inherent limitations in the nature of the tariff of the early 19th century, which served to control the growth and distribution of wealth and population. As the principal source of national revenue the tariff could not be raised too high without shutting out imports and impoverishing the exchequer. It could not be raised too high without discouraging the development of manufactures abroad.

The reciprocal advantages of foreign trade tended to disappear as an increasing number of countries attained to a large measure of self-sufficiency in manufactures and increased their surplus for export. The governments of these countries were not slow in levying directly upon the growing profits of industry. Direct taxes were first employed to supplement customs. In time they supplanted customs as the principal source of revenue.

In 1910, when the expenditures of the Federal Government of the United States were below the billion dollar mark, custom receipts accounted for more than half the total revenue. Today the income tax, personal and corporate, provides more than half the revenue, while customs account for less than one-sixth of the total.

The tariff as a minor source of revenue fails as a limitation upon the rate of industrial expansion. It fails as a limitation in this country and abroad. Any loss of revenue, from an undue increase in tariff rates, can be offset by an increase in income taxes. But these direct taxes must come from industrial expansion at home. With each nation expanding to the limit, the rate of expansion naturally eludes attention. We close our eyes to the consequences.

The problem of the tariff is further complicated, because the inherent limitations that formerly existed in the nature of direct taxation are gone. Both direct and indirect taxation are employed to increase volume and reduce costs; to encourage expansion to the limit.

DIRECT TAXATION NO LONGER BRAKE ON EXPANSION

The taxation systems of the first half of the 19th century served as brakes upon industrial expansion. Representation was attended with financial responsibility. Wealth exercised a restraining influence on the growth of population.

Prior to the general use of power machinery, there was a close relationship between the growth and distribution of wealth and population. Wealth consisted, in large part, of land and buildings, agricultural implements, and live stock. The capital-labor ratio employed in working the land was very much the same the world over.

There were certain countries, however, sufficiently advanced in agricultural practices to warrant the conclusion that the proportion of land to labor was susceptible of control. In other words—"The degree of productiveness of land and labor depended upon their being in proportion to one another." This belief found its way into the various systems of taxation of the day, and was commonly known as proportional representation and taxation.

The growth and distribution of wealth and taxation so closely paralleled each other in the early history of this country that they were recognized as interchangeable measures of progress and development. This relationship was commonly known as the rule of coincidence. The framers of the Constitution of the United States depended upon it in correlating representation and taxation. It was employed to secure the accumulated property in the States against the vote of mere numbers. Congress was empowered under this rule to levy direct taxes in accordance with the growth and distribution of wealth and population. If at any time this rule of taxation was not in just proportion to the wealth and population of the several states, Congress had the power to adopt such rule or ratio, as would bear a more direct proportion to the relative wealth and population of the states.

The rapid growth of commerce and manufactures during the 19th century destroyed this relationship between taxation and representation. The growth of mercantile and industrial capital was attended by a migration from the land to industrial centers. The movement of so many people away from the land, and the concentration of so much wealth and so many people in manufacturing centers disturbed the old-time ratio of productiveness between land and labor.

Under the new conditions one state might be three times as wealthy as another state, and still have the same population, the same representation.

Power machinery and technological improvements were contributing to a revolutionary change in the ratio of productiveness between land and labor. But it was more than a revolutionary change in agriculture. Manufacturing, commerce, and mining all increased their capital structure and decreased their labor requirements. Volume was increased at every turn and unit costs reduced. The American farmer of seventy-five years ago had his hands full in taking care of twelve crop acres. Today he can handle thirty-four. The United States Department of Commerce estimates that the output per worker for the four branches of industry, agriculture, mining, manufacturing, railway transportation, was nearly 30 per cent greater in 1925 than in 1919.

Instead of adopting a rule for the basic industries that would account for a higher degree of productiveness between wealth and labor, the United States and other industrial countries discarded proportional representation and taxation.

Capital and labor are multiplying today independently of each other; independently of any law of economy. The law of their fecundity is the law of expansion to the limit. Bloc control of taxation has been substituted for proportional taxation. These blocs employ progressive taxation to redistribute wealth at the top. Our attention is thus distracted from the real problem of effecting a better distribution of income at the source. The purchasing power of labor lacks stability because of this faulty distribution of income. Labor looks increasingly to the government for assistance. In the end industry pays for this aid twice over.

We are willing enough in this country to agree that there is a proportion between wealth and population which cannot be disturbed by the influx of too many foreigners. When it comes to safeguarding all industry against the growth of excess capacity and falling standards of living, nothing is done. We allow excess capacity to pile up and destroy profits, destroy competition, and calmly look upon this destruction as if it had always been a part of the system. Industry pitted against industry, nation against nation, in a ruthless economic war to gain every cent of income for expansion.

And the governments are backing up industry to the limit with their powers of taxation. Surely the men and women who died in the World War would turn in their graves if they knew what we were doing with our opportunities.

PROFITS NO LONGER BRAKE ON EXPANSION

Labor as well as capital is responsible for idle capacity. For a time they both benefited by increasing production and wages, by expanding markets, and reducing costs. Labor claimed that its standards might be lowered, even with high money wages, if it did not share proportionately with capital in the results of increased production. Capital, realizing that labor's buying power was essential to mass consumption, favored, in this country particularly, the high-wage, low-cost theory of production and consumption.

High wages constituted an actual share in the profits of industry. They were paid out to labor before the products of industry were sold. This placed capital at a growing disadvantage, because labor's share of profits bore no definite relation to its responsibilities for losses. Capital could not control the rate of industrial expansion, could not prevent overproduction, without the assistance of labor.

CORPORATION PROFITS NO LONGER BRAKE ON EXPANSION

The right to share in the profits of most corporations is a property right attended with limited responsibilities. Stockholders as a rule are liable for debts to the extent of their holdings.

This responsibility of ownership has of late years been all but dissipated. Stockholders, under the new conditions, are powerless to prevent overproduction. American corporations continue to plow back close to half their profits, regardless of overproduction.

The legislatures and courts have sanctioned the separation of voting power from the ownership of stock. They have sanctioned the division of common stock into voting and nonvoting classes. These changes have made it possible for the voting stock to be held by a small group of stockholders who make no proportional contribution of capital.

The high wages paid by stockholders to employes constitue a share in the results of increased production, a share in profits. These profits are paid to employes before the products of the corporation are sold. They are paid to employes without the assumption of any definite share of responsibility for losses attending overproduction.

Our anti-trust laws of the last century were directed against a restriction of production in order to maintain prices. The tendency of recent years has been to construe the law in the interest of consolidations that would increase production and reduce prices.

The difficulty with this interpretation of the law is that corporations or other forms of business organization tend to grow unwieldy as their size increases. There are limits to the number of units of capital and labor that can pull together. Many corporations have been forced to split up because they were overextended. Often large corporations operate at a higher cost than the smaller ones. The difference in cost of operation is illustrated in some of the studies of the Federal Trade Commission.

If there are limits to the rate of industrial expansion; limits beyond which we cannot go without insuring overproduction, then there must be limits to the number as well as the size of the business units that can continue to operate in any field at a fair income return.

It would be disastrous to conclude that large-scale production is suited to all industries. It would be equally disastrous to conclude that large business units cannot operate to better advantage in such industries as coal, oil, iron and steel, railroads, telephone, etc.

What we are after is a principle which will enable us to

distinguish where the advantages of large-scale and small-scale production and distribution begin and end.

UNEMPLOYMENT—FORCING EXPANSION

Industry is employing an increasing proportion of wage earners and capital as reserve. This reserve capacity is maintained with a view to taking advantage of new high peaks of demand.

But the wage earners of the industrial countries are levying upon industry indirectly through the income tax, so that there is no escaping the cost of unemployment, as was the case before the income tax came into general use.

A great deal has been said of late years about the growth of the capital structure of industry, and the loss involved in any cessation of operations.

When we take into account the purchasing power of labor, we cannot escape the fact that the temporary employment of a growing proportion of wage earners renders the purchasing power of labor more uncertain.

Each American wage earner that has had a public school education, represents an investment of many thousands of dollars. The Department of Labor figures the cost of raising a child in the $2500-a-year group at a round figure of $7238 inclusive, from birth to eighteen years.

When overproduction prevents the wage earner from realizing on this investment, society as well as the individual pays for this idleness. The interest charges on the labor investment continue whether labor works or not.

While the increased output of the United States has been attended by a steady decrease in labor requirements, many of the displaced workers have been absorbed by the new-born industries, or have been forced to accept part-time employment. If we could count on the absorption process continuing indefinitely, all would be well, but as Mr. William Green, President of the American Federation of Labor has pointed out, "sooner or later this absorption is bound to reach a point of saturation." Other nations are multiplying their productive capacity and increasing their efficiency.

During the last nine years, the total registered unemployed in Great Britain has never fallen below the million mark. The number of registered unemployed in January, 1929, for Great Britain was 1,456,737; for Germany 2,246,278; for Italy 461,889; for Austria 275,405; for Poland 160,843. Unemployment is high in Sweden as compared with pre-war standards. Preliminary census figures on unemployment in the United States, indicate that there were 2,508,151 out of a job and looking for work in April, 1930.

In 1928 the British Industrial Transference Board reported on excess capacity in the coal industry of Great Britain. The Board found that there were at least 200,000 miners permanently out of a job, and that a similar situation existed in other industries.

Great Britain exports about one-third of her coal output. During the first thirteen years of the 20th century there was an annual increase in output of 62,000,000 tons. This increase was attended by rising costs of production and decreasing returns.

The rapid industrialization of the rest of the world has reduced the world demand for English textiles, metallurgical wares, and coal, which formerly made up the bulk of her trade.

England finds herself hampered by old-fashioned industrial plants; hampered by the cost of idle capacity. That she needs to reorganize her basic industries (including agriculture), is only too apparent. But the $300,000,000 a year that are being paid out in doles stand in the way of reorganization. It would seem that from two to five million people will have to migrate, if English industry is to be afforded the necessary opportunity for reorganization. Without this opportunity the rate of industrial expansion cannot be brought into balance with the growth of income.

There are other nations, such as Germany, Italy, India, Japan, that must be relieved of their excess man power if they are to bring their rate of industrial expansion under control. Their need for territory should afford England and the other colonial powers an opportunity to dispose of some of their holdings at a fair consideration. This will aid England in financing the development of her much-needed migration centers.

In growing up to their excess capacity, the nations of the East and West will undoubtedly find it necessary to introduce part-time employment as a condition of industry. As the nations bring their rate of expansion under control, the industries will be afforded an opportunity to work out of part-time employment. The logical, sensible, and only final answer to technological unemployment, says Mr. Stuart Chase in July *Harper's,* is to shorten the working hours, "Why not keep the entire force on the payroll but work them less?"

A SUMMARY OF THE FACTS—OVERPRODUCTION

Overproduction is no longer an isolated problem, confined to particular industries or nations. The extensive use of power machinery and technological improvements has greatly increased the productive power of industry, as well as its expansive power.

Productive capacity is increasing at a rate out of proportion to the slower growth of buying and consuming capacity. We are producing more goods today than income can absorb. Under these conditions the American farmers find that seven hundred million bushels of wheat bring more money than a billion bushels. And nine million bales of cotton are worth more in return to the producers than thirteen million bales.

Curiously enough, the individual manufacturer to avoid the evils of overproduction in his own plant often expands his productive facilities when the law of supply and demand operates to reduce his markets. He does this because he knows that when there is more than enough of a certain product on the market he can only dispose of his if the price is lower than that of his competitor. In order to make his price lower he employs technological improvements and machinery; he increases his output to secure lower production costs. Naturally, however, his competitors all do likewise and a situation originally bad grows worse.

Volume production and distribution have forced down the cost of production and forced up wages to a point which compels industry to expand to the limit. Wasteful producers and distributors are encouraged to enter the competitive field, regardless of their influence on standards of production. Industry is forced to anticipate new high peaks for an ever-expanding volume capacity. Reserve capacity is maintained on an ever-increasing scale, in a vain attempt to take advantage of these peaks, in a vain attempt to control production, prices, and markets.

But consumption cannot catch up with production as of old, because reserve capacity is increasing faster than consuming capacity. Modern business is powerless to take normal requirements into account. And yet we know within well-defined limits the annual requirements for basic commodities like coal, cotton, steel, lumber, wheat, oil, food, clothing, etc.

This inability to gear production to normal requirements is forcing industry to sell below cost; below the cost of upkeep of the capital-labor investment. It is forcing cut-throat competition between industries and nations. The gap between supply and demand grows wider and wider.

The World War gave a final push to the overproduction movement. Nations were unduly encouraged to develop home

industries, home markets, and a surplus for export. Those
nations that were accustomed to export before the war have
increased their capacity with a view to lowering prices and
winning back trade in the restricted markets of the world.
Back of the glut of world markets today is this reserve capacity
of the nations. If it were brought into general use price levels
would disappear.

The analysis of the situation by the contributors to this
symposium discussion cannot fail to make anyone casually
interested in overproduction question the direction of our present course. The economic world is at the crossroads. Overproduction is a common problem.

There is so close a relationship today between basic industries, that overproduction in one industry induces overproduction in other industries. The overexpansion of cotton acreage
insures the overexpansion of cotton spindles. Overproduction
of automobiles insures idle capacity in the steel mills. The
overexpansion of oil wells insures an excessive number of filling stations. Waste in production insures waste in distribution
and consumption.

Overproduction—the capacity to produce consistently more
goods than income can absorb—has its origin in the rate of
industrial expansion. It is only too evident from a review of
the forces making for expansion, that we have a new high-
power machinery of production, energized by the labor of a
billion and more human beings and a billion horsepower.

This machinery of production is being operated without
brakes or governor, to keep adjusted the rates at which basic
industries are growing; without brakes or governor to insure
the productive growth and distribution of wealth, income, and
population.

Wealth and population are multiplying independently of
each other; independently of any law of economy. The law
of their fecundity is the law of expansion to the limit. The

same law operating in the animal and plant kingdoms, determines the evolutionary range of plants and animals.

Charles Darwin and A. H. Wallace saw in this tendency the essential cause of the struggle for existence. They saw that the various forms of plant and animal life would overrun the world were it not for the fact that only a few in each generation survive.

The mortality rate of population and wealth (growth of excess capacity), is the determining factor today in man's struggle for existence. This destructive rate of growth of population and wealth will establish the limits of our evolutionary range, unless we bring the capacity to produce and consume into balance.

XIX

CONSTRUCTIVE PROPOSALS

MANY of the contributors to this symposium suggest means and ways of leveling out the peaks and valleys of capital-labor employment, with a view to preventing overproduction. While the plans differ in many minor respects, there is general agreement on the fundamental cause and cure of overproduction. Supply and demand are out of alignment. The facts and figures required for sound judgment are lacking. Modern business has grown too complicated for guesswork or rule-of-thumb methods. Let us consider some of the suggestions already made.

OIL

Without conservation, says Sir Henri Deterding, the oil industry will continue to bring in new producing fields before they are needed; price wars will continue; oil profits will disappear.

Conservation will eliminate the evils of overproduction; discourage the multiplication of wasteful producers; discourage the exhaustion of one producing field at the expense of another.

President Hoover and the Department of the Interior advise the unit development of the oil fields, with a view to sinking wells only where necessary. Under these conditions oil will not be produced until provision has been made for utilizing gas, and there is a proper market for the gas and oil. The proceeds will be divided among the owners in proportion to their holdings. The idea seems to have made considerable progress in California.

The Petroleum Institute has endorsed the enactment of laws to permit agreements between operators in a single pool for the orderly development of oil and gas holdings.

At the present time, says Mr. Salisbury, the earnings of the oil industry in the United States cannot be sufficient without a larger measure of cooperative effort in the balancing of production and demand.

AGRICULTURE

The surplus, says Dr. Baker, continues to be the great problem in American Agriculture. The farmers continue to produce more than they can sell at a profit. On the one side of the Pacific millions of people, mostly farmers and their families, are often hungry and sometimes perish of starvation, while on the other side of the ocean less than one-tenth as many farmers are producing more food and fibres than the people of the Continent can consume, and are suffering from a surplus. The problem of the Orient, even more than in Europe, is that of developing the purchasing power of the people.

In the United States a great deal of marginal and sub-marginal land is used for crops, instead of for timber growing and grazing. This use of marginal land discourages the use of more fertilizer. One way of improving the situation, concludes Dr. Baker, is through a new national land policy. The national Government and the States should make a classification of our land resources. This definite information concerning the physical characteristics of the land would indicate the true course to be followed. It would discourage the use of marginal and sub-marginal land for crops.

Too much thought, says Dr. Lipman, cannot be given to a most thorough-going study of land utilization policies, the protection of our soils against erosion and chemical denudation, the elimination of marginal acres as a competitive factor.

THE COTTON TEXTILE INDUSTRY

The use of marginal land for cotton growing, insures overproduction. Too much cotton insures too many spindles.

Balancing production more nearly with consumption, says Mr. Kendall, requires strenuous measures, and calls for a type of cooperation to which the industry is not habituated but which it is coming to recognize as a first essential to restoration of equilibrium.

Together with the reduction of hours of work for operatives and maintenance of wages—lifting the industry out of the long-hour, low-wage group—other measures are necessary if a more normal balance between production and demand is to be assured. The industry needs more merchandising; more research; more emphasis on creation; more acceptance of the modern, scientific attitude toward business..

WOOL INDUSTRY

Overproduction as a menace, concludes Mr. Whiteside, can only be eliminated through the coordination of industry in first obtaining the data required on which to base its operations, and secondly, to set up the mechanism to educate the individual organizations in the industry to realize the meaning of the facts when available.

The question of methods to be adopted to prevent overproduction is the most important single subject for economic and political consideration in the world today.

Statistics are absolutely essential if goods are to be marketed at a fair price; if each seller is to know his exact position in the industry; if the style service is to be adequate; if a physical mechanism is to be acquired with which to determine and adminster the policies of the industry as a whole.

SILK INDUSTRY

In order to create a normal condition that will insure a more reliable basis of operation in the silk industry, manufacturers feel that they must make a closer study of what is being sold and to what extent. Then must come an application of that study to their inventories.

Further than that, says Mr. Hill, the industry must find an answer to the problem of adjustment of mass production, to a product controlled by style. A closer study, however, of their current markets, and an application of that information to their products, will, it is believed, point the way for the constructively thinking silk manufacturer and distributor.

RAYON INDUSTRY

What can be done by rayon producers to alleviate periods of business advance and recession, dispose of the problem of over-production, and give stability to profits? What may other business agencies do to attain this same end?

Mr. Bassill offers the following suggestions:

Cooperation on the part of the rayon industry as a whole in furnishing its members, as well as others who are interested, with complete and comprehensive figures on the amount of rayon produced, sold, and held in stock. Producers should analyze their sales and the sales of the industry so as to determine the extent and direction of a cyclical variation in sales; so as to anticipate cyclical periods.

A slight depression is, after all, much more desirable than a severe one. The Federal Reserve Board can contribute to the stabilization of production by tightening credit when business begins to go above normal. It is believed that the answer to "What is Normal," can be satisfactorily determined once there is a specific demand for a more even keel in business.

Some plan should be worked out for business groups so that

they could attempt to control overproduction, both individually and collectively.

In conclusion it would seem that there must be an extensive, popular, and consistent demand for business stability before the problem of overproduction in industry can be intelligently approached and solved. Such a demand is now present in all branches of business from capital to labor. It is interesting to note, however, that this desire is commonly expressed only during such periods of extreme depression as are now being witnessed; during periods of normal business or in times of so-called prosperity, the cry is no longer heard.

COAL INDUSTRY

The precise need of the bituminous industry, says Mr. Bockus, is the right to secure, by cooperative action, the continuous adjustment of the production of bituminous coal to the existing demand for it, thereby discouraging wasteful methods of production and consumption and making possible its production under conditions that will insure the welfare of its employees and the prosperity of its operating companies.

As mine mechanization can be applied only to mines of some size, and as its effect is to increase the capacity of such mines, the result of the mine mechanization movement will be a tendency toward the elimination of small mines and the concentration of coal production in fewer and larger companies. Such increase in the size of operating units should have a direct bearing upon the possibility of applying remedies to the existing condition of price depression. It will reenforce the already existing advantages of large-scale operation which bituminous mining shares with many other industries.

Being deprived of the right to practice adequate self-regulation, the industry is attempting to improve conditions as far as possible through cooperative agreements to abandon harmful practices. These agreements are embodied in codes of ethics. By the adoption of such codes of ethics and their observance some restraint may be placed upon the cut-throat competitive practices of an industry. However, so long as the anti-trust laws remain unchanged nothing can be embodied in those codes which provides for either the cooperative regulation of production or prices or for the division of territory.

STEEL INDUSTRY

Every effort should be made to carry on the vast volume of construction work in this country at a fairly even rate. The present volume of seven billion dollars (all construction) furnishes employment to three million people. The industry is one of the largest consumers of steel.

In the wild scramble for volume, says Mr. Abbott, all our basic industries must learn that distress lurks just ahead, and the only remedy lies in the rationalization of output to consumption. Industry has yet to develop a method of regulating production to consuming capacity.

We are forbidden by the anti-trust laws to advise competitors as to selling prices. However, might we not feasibly advise each other as to the expansion of productive capacity, without running foul of these laws?

RADIO INDUSTRY

During the first six months of 1929, says Major Frost, the radio industry sold 1,500,000 sets, or approximately one million more sets than during the corresponding period of 1928. This large increase in sales encouraged many manufacturers to plan production programs for five times this number of sets for the last half of 1929.

Radio has arrived and taken its place with the other great American industries. We face, however, with these industries the task of bringing potential output into closer relation with normal demand. The accumulation on a national scale of a margin of excess capacity, is far different from the accumulation of temporary surpluses. Temporary surpluses lend themselves to absorption. Idle capacity is a continual drag. It encourages wasteful producers and distributors to enter the field, regardless of the ability of existing manufacturers, wholesalers and retailers to care for the demand. Before encouraging further expansion, let us secure an approximate idea of the potential capacity of the radio industry.

INTERNATIONAL TRADE

With fast and cheap transportation, and the auxiliary aids of the international telegraph, radio, and telephone services, the world is rapidly becoming contracted into one large market. Under these conditions, explains Mr. Chalmers, the need is likely to become increasingly urgent, not only for full and prompt information as to conditions of crops, stocks, prices, and requirements all over the world, but for well-laid plans for such control or direction of production in each country that there will be better adjustment of production to demand. It is hardly conceivable that the producers and traders in the various countries will much longer tolerate, without earnest efforts at prevention or at least mitigation, the present unplanned and uncoordinated conditions of international markets, that has been resulting in alternate periods of shortage and high prices at one time and overproduction and depressed prices at another. The effort to attain such a balance of production to market demand, which has been one of the prime objectives of the current movement for international cartels among European producers, may be the forerunner of more extended efforts, in varying forms, towards a better international adjustment of supply and demand.

A review of America's place in world commerce a century ago and now furnishes a rough measure of the rate of industrial expansion attained. This rate of expansion is a factor of the first importance in charting our future course.

ADVERTISING

Consumers, explains Mr. Fassnacht, cannot long spend more than they can earn; if they are to eat more, wear more, travel more and generally consume more they must earn more.

Overproduction directly cuts down income. Throughout the world, therefore, the business man should have the ardent support and enthusiastic cooperation of the advertising man in any battle to overcome a condition that menaces standards of living.

If, in the past, advertising men have plunged their clients into an expansion at home and abroad without proper analysis of consumer's ability to buy, in the future we must see a change in such policies.

The successful advertising agency of the future will continue to do more than invent snappy slogans and create pretty pictures. It will be a marketing organization approaching the whole problem of advertising from the economic angle. Business men the world over must inevitably arrive at a satisfactory way to control expansion and to preserve that balance between growth of productive capacity and growth of national income essential to prosperity and rising standards of living. It will increasingly become a primary function of the advertising agency to originate marketing methods and merchandising plans that fully account for all factors involved in problems of stabilization.

MARKETING

The problem of excess capacity is not confined to production. In retail distribution operations, says Mr. Cherington, the real menace is the danger of allowing the business to be too small to pay the price of managerial ability. Many independent merchants are willing to do business for less than $23.00 a week net profit. But the cost to them, and to society, of their continuing to operate below the minimum scale for

competent retailing is one phase of the economics of merchandise distribution which has been neglected.

We have still to find the size and number of business units best
suited to the various branches of production and distribution. In
the case of railroads, telephones, oil refineries, steel rolling mills,
and other enterprises, the continuous search for the optimum scale
has led into larger operating units.

Given the scale of operations best suited to the various
industries, the task of adjusting production to market requirements will be much simplified. Without this scale
potential capacity cannot be accurately measured. Wasteful
producers are encouraged to increase.

UNIFICATION

There has been an astonishing increase, says Mr. Sisson, in
the size of our industrial and financial units. It was less
than fifty years ago that the realization of the gains to be
derived from an elimination of competition began to find
expression in the formation of consolidations, trusts, and
cartels. Concentration of control has become the order of
the day. The essential soundness of mass production and
distribution has been demonstrated.

Different branches of economic effort profit from unification in
different ways and in different degrees. In some lines the urge is
much stronger than in others. But, in one way or another, industry, commerce, transportation, communication, finance, and
even agriculture are following the trend.

For the automatic regulation that free competition has always
provided, must be substituted an artificial regulation dependent on
human wisdom and foresight, and subject to the weakness of
human nature.

The age of big business is here to stay. Our problem is not to
hinder its development, but to promote it and direct it in such a

way as to reap its full benefits without suffering from its possible evils.

LIMITS TO MERGER TREND

Mergers and consolidations, says Dr. Jordan, have not proved, and are not likely to prove, a cure-all for excess capacity, overproduction, or cut-throat competition.

The tendency towards industrial concentration through mergers has resulted in the protection and maintenance of the interests of the unsuccessful marginal independents which are absorbed. The result is to lower the margin of profit and bring new marginal producers into the field.

Despite the fact that the most modern developments in the use of electric power permit a wider distribution of purchasing power and better access to local markets, these advantages have been almost wholly ignored, because of a belief in the superior profitableness of large scale, concentrated production.

In order to secure a better balance between production and consumption it is necessary somehow to supplement our system of consumer credit through which purchasing power can be advanced to consumers somewhat ahead of productive activity.

MANAGEMENT AS A CONSTRUCTIVE FACTOR

Modern industry is too complicated, it is expanding too rapidly to rely on rule-of-thumb methods. The rates at which basic industries are growing cannot be kept in adjustment unless the rates are known.

Scientific management furnishes the technique for making the measurements. Time and motion studies are essential to the working out of standard ratios of productiveness for the basic industries.

The principal objective of scientific management, says Dr. Person, has been the regularized increase in the industrial power of the individual plant. The application of this science to entire industries is known as rationalization.

The principles of the science establish in place of management which is highly opportunistic, speculative, and unregulated; that which is predetermined and controlled. They involve the measurement of industrial conditions and tendencies and of the state of market demands. They provide for a schedule of growth which is fairly even, and will avoid the overextension in times of boom, and serious retrenchment in times of depression.

If all industrial enterprises were inspired to employ the science of management, overproduction would be so reduced as practically to disappear as a serious problem. It may require some great emotional reaction to some greater crisis in our industrial life than we have yet experienced, to generate a general impulse toward an art of managing which will take advantage of what we have already learned about the science of management.

"UNDERCONSUMPTION"

Messers. Foster and Catchings have also given profound attention to the problem of overproduction. They contend that the present industrial dilemma is due to a producing capacity in excess of visible consumption, or "underconsumption."

As industry is now financed the flow of money to consumers does not keep pace with the flow of goods; and without a full flow of money into consumption there cannot be a full flow of goods into consumption. As business expands and profits are realized, approximately half the profits are used to produce more goods. Thus the flow of goods which consumers must buy if business is to prosper increases more rapidly than the flow of money to consumers.

They suggest that the way out of the dilemma of thrift is to stimulate consumer buying by paying "higher real wages" —decreasing the risks of business by increasing the range and realiability of economic measurements—speeding up work on public buildings and roads and other government facilities, so as to relieve or avert unemployment.

A SPECIFIC PROPOSAL BY THE EDITOR

In addition to the above suggestions, the editor of this volume begs leave to submit a concrete proposal which perhaps goes even farther.

A compelling motive is essential to the balancing of producing and consuming capacity. Exhortations to slow down expansion, to plant fewer acres, to reduce the supply of sugar, rubber, coffee, nitrates, are of little avail as long as the motive is lacking.

If it pays to waste we waste. When it pays to conserve we will conserve.

The cost of carrying excess capacity no longer pays for itself. Hence the need of a motive for labor and investment that will penalize overproduction and place a premium on a more regular business advancement.

The substitution of *income* as a motive for labor and investment in place of profits, will afford the needed compulsion. By requiring capital and labor to be brought into use in due proportion to each other, the compelling motive will be further strengthened. By establishing a limit to the income return the rate of growth of population and wealth will be subjected to control. *New resources will be kept out of use until they are needed.*

A fair income return on each standard unit of investment will constitute the desired balance; the desired balance between producing and consuming capacity; the desired balance between the rate of growth of income and the rate of industrial expansion.

Carried into the structure and organization of corporations, this principle will serve as the basis for distributing advantages and responsibilities between stockholders and the investors of labor. The preservation of a balance between the rate of corporate expansion and the rate of income growth will bring its reward. Overproduction will bring its penalty.

LABOR AS AN INVESTMENT

Under the new conditions, labor as well as capital will constitute an investment bearing a fixed overhead. Assumption of responsibility for its proportion of the overhead will entitle labor to a vested interest in income. Capital and labor will both be responsible for meeting the cost of upkeep in advance of expansion, in advance of a division of income. The investor of labor, who consistently produces above a minimum, above the overhead on his job, will share income with capital. He will share in proportion to his contribution to income.

The minimum wage return paid to the capital and labor investors will be paid on a standard of performance. This standard or ratio of productiveness will be worked out for each basic industry through time and motion studies. It will be sufficiently high to cover the cost of upkeep of the standard unit of investment.

Through the graphic representation of the overhead attached to the job, the individual employe will gain a new insight into the workings of his particular business. He will be held responsible for checking his daily production against the overhead attached to his job.

This close analytical study of the job will enable the workman to gain from day to day an approximate idea of his contribution to production. With a proportional interest in income he will be constantly on the alert to prevent any action or inaction, which will deprive him of his rightful share.

Under the profit motive there is little incentive for foremen to become acquainted with the overhead costs of the department in which they work. Most employes remain ignorant of the overhead attached to the job. They see the profits, they know something about the prices secured for the finished product, but they fail to know what part of the selling price goes towards meeting the expenses on the selling end, for insurance, interest, depreciation, taxes, etc. They have no idea of the overhead attached to the jobs higher up.

STANDARD RATIO OF INVESTMENT

Each basic industry will work out its standard ratio of capital-labor investment, and secure the final approval of the government. In the United States the initial studies might very well be carried out under the direction of the Taylor Society and the American Standards Association, with the assistance of the American Federation of Labor and the various trade organizations of the country.

These standards will be gradually brought into alignment, so that eventually all industries will be giving an equivalence of performance, for a similar income return. They will be brought into alignment so that eventually all standards can be raised together.

The outside limit of the income return will be the same for all industries. This control over maximum earnings will enable the standard ratios of performance to be brought into alignment. It will prevent new capital-labor resources from being brought into use at a rate destructive of existing standards.

The maximum income return will be fixed by the government at whatever rate is required to insure the productive growth and distribution of wealth, income, and population. We may find that an income return of 7 per cent on the standard of investment is too high in this country. In any event the limit will be subject to revision, downwards or upwards, possibly every five or ten years.

PRINCIPLE OF BALANCE APPLIED TO CORPORATE CONTROL

Under such a plan, each department of a corporation will constitute a fraction of the total capital-labor investment; a fraction organized for production. Each department will be represented in the directorate. The basis of representation in the lower branch of the directorate will be the capital-labor ratio of investment for the particular industry. Each department will be represented in the upper branch on the basis of a unit of income. This unit will constitute the income return allowed on the standard unit of investment. If the ratio is ten thousand dollars of labor investment to twenty thousand dollars of capital investment, with a maximum income return of 8 per cent, the unit of representation in the upper branch will be $2400 of income.

Representation in the two branches of the directorate will thus be employed to effect a balance between the rate of income growth and the rate of corporate expansion. *The desired balance will constitute a standard income return on each unit of investment.*

The department that fails to realize a balance between its rate of expansion and its rate of income growth, will unduly increase its overhead and decrease its representation. Representation will thus be employed to penalize waste, prevent overexpansion and encourage the extended use of the resources employed.

The directorate will be responsible for dividing income between the capital and labor investors. The proportion going to the labor investment will be divided between the departments in accordance with their contribution to income. Department heads will be responsible for dividing the income accruing to the labor investment between those investors who consistently produce above a minimum, above the overhead costs on their job.

Directors of corporations will be paid in accordance with their contribution to production. Their jobs will call for a standard of performance.

ADVANTAGES OF INCOME MOTIVE

The advantages that will attend such a substitution of income as a motive for labor and investment are numerous and far-reaching. Mention of a few of the advantages will give some idea of what the change would mean to you and me.

Elimination of the class struggle is the first item on the list. There will no longer be a wage-earning and a profit-earning class. Both capital and labor will be wage-earners. Both will have a vested interest in income. This interest in income will make labor as well as capital responsible for preventing overproduction. The energy that is spent today in the struggle for maximum wages and profits will be expended in preventing overproduction; in raising the income level all along the line.

By helping to stabilize the flow of income, labor will insure itself against a fall in living standards, against wasted effort and premature old age.

Under the stimulus of the income motive the human factors contributing to all-around superiority will be brought to the fore. Reward and effect will be more closely related. Each investor of labor will work with the knowledge that his best effort is being taken into account from day to day. The channels of contact between each dollar of capital and labor investment and the whole concern will be kept open.

The division of income between the capital and labor investors will be a constant reminder that idle machinery or idle men is an unproductive charge that must come out of income. It will help to stabilize consumer buying power. Both capital and labor will be responsible for timing expansion so that, "the flow of money into expansion will keep pace with the flow of goods into consumption."

By discontinuing the practice of directly financing betterments from earnings; by eliminating the distribution of shares of stock as a bonus to encourage the purchase of bonds; as a means of financing construction, a close correspondence can be secured between the par value of security issues and the actual investment. This correspondence is essential if the valuation of the capital-labor investment is to be kept up to date. It is essential to the measurement of the rate of industrial expansion or contraction.

The facts required to measure the rate of industrial expansion need to be secured from each investor of capital and labor. Income provides the motive. These facts can be tabulated by all producing and distributing units and reported at regular intervals to local government agencies. These agencies will make the facts and figures on industrial expansion generally available. Private research organizations will help to interpret this information. Without this knowledge we cannot hope to bring the rate of industrial expansion under control; we cannot hope to substitute sound judgment for guesswork and rule-of-thumb.

Carried into the organization and control of business, the principle of balance will serve as an index to the number and size of the business units that can continue to operate in any field at a standard income return. It will indicate where the economies of large-scale and small-scale operations begin and end. It will furnish an approximate idea of how many units of capital and labor can pull together.

Relieved of the fear of destructive competition, business will no longer be justified in withholding the financial set-up from either the labor or capital investors. In his study of corporation profits, L. H. Sloan found that the majority of corporations in this country make public no data whatsoever to inform their security holders as to the amount of profit that is appropriated for the depreciation charges and reserves each year.

The speeding up of work on public buildings and roads is temporary relief for overproduction and unemployment. All our basic industries are overexpanded. The difference between the rate of growth of income and the rate of industrial expansion is the measure of this excess capacity. It is the measure of the inflation of modern industrial values. The losses of deflation can be reduced to a minimum, if we bring our rate of industrial expansion under control and grow up to this excess capacity.

As the motive for labor and investment determines in large part the character of property; the substitution of the income motive will change the character of all forms of property. Income will compel us to look to the extended use of the property employed, rather than to its immediate exploitation. Income, not profits, will serve as the ultimate source of farm values, of all industrial values.

Legally obligated to treat income as the measure of property values; legally obligated to limit the return; legally obligated to meet the cost of upkeep in advance of expansion, capital and labor will hesitate to bring more coal mines, more acres of land, more oil wells, more distributing agencies, more labor into use than will allow of a standard income return on the investment.

IN CONCLUSION

We have a new high-power machinery of production at our command. Operated with brakes and governor, we can avoid drastic business recessions; avoid what has always been looked upon as the inevitable law of the rise and fall of nations.

This machinery of production has brought into view a new objective which is all inclusive enough to allay strife. Today the desire for what the economist calls "higher standards of living" is universal.

The brakes and governor on the older machinery were discarded as the newer machinery of production was brought into use. No particular attention was paid to their elimination until the World War made us suddenly realize that something was fundamentally wrong with the new mechanism. Millions of lives were sacrificed, but we did not stop to examine the cause.

There were not many who saw that the machinery of production had gotten out of hand, that a collision was inevitable. There are more people today who realize that the war did not lead us to construct an adequate braking system or a governor for the new high-power machinery of production. They know that the machinery of production is uncontrolled; that the very tendency which brought on the war was aggravated by the war; that we are in the midst of a trade war that has no parallel in human history. They know that unless this economic war between industries and nations is ended, the cost of war will continue to increase. In other words, we cannot enjoy rising standards of living and war. One or the other must go.

World production and world consumption are out of alignment. The gap between production and consumption grows wider. Overproduction is forcing industry to expand to the limit in anticipation of new high peaks of demand. We assume that because a certain increase in volume has netted a fair return in the past, that a similar increase in volume will continue to net the same return. Capitalization is fixed on the basis of this anticipated return. Credit is extended on the increase in value of properties which serve as collateral securities.

The plant capacity back of this ever-increasing volume

eludes measurement. More and more of the earnings that belong in the upkeep account go into expansion. Producers and distributors have information regarding the volume of sales, but lack information as to the rate of expansion of competitors, or other industries. The same is true of nations.

The rates at which basic industries are growing cannot very well be kept in adjustment as long as the rates elude measurement. And the rates cannot be measured unless they are subject to control; unless the cost of upkeep is met by capital and labor in advance of expansion.

For many years past the return on money invested in agriculture has been relatively smaller than the return on money invested in commercial and manufacturing enterprises. This difference has given manufacturing and commerce a world lead over agriculture. It has made for the unbalanced development of the three basic world industries.

The nations of the East cannot employ manufacturing and commerce to advantage because any increase in income is usually absorbed, not by a rise in standards of living, but by an increase in population. They have built up an excess capacity in man power which stands in the way of the profitable development of manufacturing and commerce.

With the aid of commerce and manufacturing the nations of the West have built up an excess capacity in horsepower. This excess capacity has brought into operation the law of diminishing income returns. Wealth and population are increasing at a much faster rate than the slower growth of income.

Some way must be found to control the rate of industrial expansion. This control is essential if the nations of the East and West are to grow up to their excess capacity, if a regular business advance is to be substituted for boom periods and drastic recessions.

All nations will not employ the same control. Some nations

do not distinguish any economy in the ownership of private property. They will very likely design their control for government use.

Those nations, on the other hand, that conceive of private property as a reward for thrift, ambition, caution, and industry; that think of it as attended with responsibilities as well as advantages, should not hesitate to employ the income motive in constructing the necessary brakes and governor.

We have built up high standards of living in this country. The best in those standards must be preserved if the level in other countries is to be raised. Clearly it is to our interest to take the initiative in a movement for "balanced prosperity"; in a movement that will encourage all nations to realize and sustain higher standards of living all along the line.

England will welcome this move; China will welcome it. No nation can doubt our sincerity in bringing our own rate of expansion under control. Such a policy will invite worldwide reciprocity.